sugar&spice

This book is for Nige, Mattie and Jake.

sugar & spice

Absolute Press

kate weatherell

First published in Great Britain in 2006 by
Absolute Press
Scarborough House
29 James Street West
Bath BA1 2BT
Phone 44 (0) 1225 316013
Fax 44 (0) 1225 445836
E-mail info@absolutepress.co.uk
Website www.absolutepress.co.uk

Text © Kate Weatherell
Photography © Jason Lowe

Publisher Jon Croft
Editor Meg Avent
Design Matt Inwood
Photography Jason Lowe
Food styling Kate Weatherell

A catalogue record of this book is available from the British Library.

ISBN 1 904573 40 1

Printed and bound by Bath Press

This book was set in ITC American Typewriter. In 1974, Joel Kaden and
Tony Stan created this proportionally spaced typeface by adapting the monospaced
designs of typewriter letter styles. Kaden designed the light and medium weights
and Stan contributed the bold weight. The typewriter was invented by
Christopher Latham Sholes in 1868.

contents

think spice

Once upon a time, spices were internationally prized and coveted. Not only were they used to flavour and preserve food, they were used as currency, fabulous gifts, medicine and aphrodisiacs, were sacrificed to gods, caused wars, divorce, murder, piracy and made some countries very wealthy indeed. But in these days of the oil-driven economy, antibiotics, fast food, monosodium glutamate and other manufactured chemical stimulants, spices have been devalued. More often than not, they suffer the humiliation of being crammed into small plastic jars, and are banished to the back of the kitchen cupboard. Neglected and lurking in the shadows of ice cream toppings, gravy granules and tomato ketchup, they lose their potency and barely get a look in. And as for 'Sugar and Spice'? In cakes, puddings and other sweet dishes, spices have commonly become an afterthought, except where they are routinely used in the likes of ginger snaps and Christmas cake.

But for those of us who enjoy remarkable ingredients and who still like picking up pans and banging around the kitchen, there is a whole mystical world to explore. Cinnamon, cloves, ginger, nutmeg, saffron and cardamom, coriander, chilli, pepper – the list goes on - each one has its own fabulous and evocative personality. Spices build bridges between and twist around other flavours. Sugar and caramel pick up and amplify the sweet edge of any spice from star anise to vanilla. They make great marriages with fruits – pear and vanilla, cherry and nutmeg, mango and five spice to name a handful. So often when you thumb through a recipe book or magazine, you find sweet recipes crying out for a touch of spice here or there. Why are spices left out, when just a tip of a teaspoon can transform a summery tart, cake, compote or pudding?

Experiment and you will find that one spice tempers another. Cardamom on its own in a dish can have an unappealing, penetrating almost detergent flavour. Add bay or cinnamon and magically, cardamom is brought back down to earth again with an aromatic lemony hum. Clove oil has been used to numb toothache. You get a sense of this if you catch one accidentally in your tooth. But in moderation, cloves add a pungent, rich and peppery edge to spice mixes in all manner of baking and of course in mulled cider, wine and beer.

This is not a book about the history of spices. I steer clear of the politics of the spice trail, the spice-embalmed bodies of the ancient Egyptians and the multitudinous biblical and Sanskrit references. Rather, this book is a tribute to the harmony of sugar and spice in sometimes surprising puddings, ices, sweets, biscuits, cakes and drinks.

how to buy, use and look after spices

Spices bought in supermarkets are generally over-priced and over-packaged and should be avoided whenever possible. Cut out several middlemen and go to any well-stocked Oriental, Asian or Middle Eastern high street store that will stock most if not all of the spices used in these recipes. These shops tend to have a good turnover, supplying both the domestic and trade markets, which promises a fresher product. They invariably offer fantastic value and tend to use a minimum of packaging. See just how much you save by buying their bags of spices. You can always split a bag with friends if you feel over-faced.

Internet spice sites can be entertaining, informative and perfect for an efficient, good value one-stop-shop for all your spices (see *shopping for spices*, page 125). Of the spices used in this book, top quality vanilla, sumac and saffron can prove the trickiest to obtain. If you don't have a local deli or supplier that you can trust, I would recommend using the internet, where numerous suppliers are vying for your business.

Don't buy ready-ground spices, because the volatile oils responsible for each spice's individual character will already have begun to evaporate. Buy whole spices and grind them yourself. Electric coffee grinders cost little more than ten pounds. Invest in one and dedicate it to grinding all of your spices. A possible exception to this rule would be dried ginger root, which if processed in a coffee grinder may yield a rather lumpy and stringy product. Fill tightly lidded jars with the aromatic dried pods, buds, kernels, sticks and seeds, stack them in a dark dry cupboard and grind as you go. Keep a tiny self-sealing bag in each jar to store any excess freshly-ground spice.

All spice quantities in the following recipes, with the exception of ginger and sumac, are based on freshly-ground quantities. If you are using bought ground spices, you will have to increase the quantities appropriately.

summer spice

Give your spice cupboard a summer airing and release your epicurean imagination. Spicing doesn't have to be confined to steamed puddings, syrupy cakes and gingerbread. There are barrel-loads of great spice-fruit relationships to be enjoyed: plums and cinnamon, pear and vanilla, rhubarb and ginger... pineapple and black pepper?

tropical fruit salad with chilli, jaggery and lime
white peaches and raspberries in chilled spiced frascati
peppered balsamic strawberry and mascarpone tart
poached pears with spiced syrup and toasted almond cream
late summer pavlova with cinnamon meringue and spiced plums
stone fruit doughnut fritters with cinnamon sugar
tarte reine-claude, lightly spiced
buttery glazed pear & vanilla tart
intense rhubarb and ginger caramel
mango and five spice tarte tatin
grilled pineapple with vodka and cracked black pepper

tropical fruit salad with chilli, jaggery and lime

This dish starts the fire, but puts it out at the same time. In Thailand, the streets are lined with food stalls and trolleys festooned with inflated plastic bags tied with coloured elastic bands. Each bag contains an extraordinary dish; squid in vicious inky sauce, jellied things with bizarre vegetables, crabs, beef, you name it. But it is the bags of the sweetest pineapple, chopped in geometric shapes and shaken with salt and chilli that have inspired this tongue-sizzling yet refreshing fruit salad.

Jaggery, which is essentially dehydrated sugar cane juice, is an Indian ingredient and one of my favourite sweeteners. It has a rich earthy caramel flavour, which is found in no other sugar. The closest relations are Thai palm sugar and Demerara.

This recipe gives you an idea of the breadth of fruits appropriate and available. But use whatever's about, and keep it simple if you prefer. Just so you know, granadilla has rather an alarming frogspawn texture, but once you've broken up the seeds, it gives a great crunch with a low-key passion fruit flavour. Yes, blueberries aren't that tropical, but they look great in any fruit salad.

75g jaggery, palm sugar, or unrefined brown sugar such as Demerara
2 tbsp water
2 medium chillies, deseeded and finely chopped
juice of 2 limes
$1/4$ tsp salt
1 small or $1/2$ large pineapple
1 large wedge watermelon
1 medium mango
2 passion fruit or 1 large granadilla
1 small punnet blueberries
8 lychees
seeds of 1 pomegranate, all bitter pith removed
1 small paw paw
handful soft mint leaves, torn (optional)

Dissolve the jaggery in the water in a small non-reactive pan over a low heat, crushing it with the back of a spoon to aid the process. Add the chopped chilli, lime juice and salt and leave to cool.

Wash, peel, deseed and slice (where appropriate) all of the fruit into bite-size pieces. Place in a large bowl, with the exception of the paw paw, which you will add last to prevent it from turning to mush.

Pour the chilli syrup over the fruit and toss the fruit to cover evenly with the chilli pieces. Add the paw paw and stir gently.

Refrigerate and eat the same day. Stir in the mint, if using, 10 minutes before serving.

serves 6–8

white peaches and raspberries in chilled spiced frascati

Dip a crisp biscotti, such as my *macadamia nut, orange and star anise biscotti* (page 89), into the light and brightly spiced fragrant liquor – only the first step in enjoying this sophisticated, clean and fresh summery dessert.

White peaches have a unique honeyed floral flavour and when peeled are left with an alluring pink blush. The white peach season used to be short, but specialist growers have managed to extend this to almost match that of the yellow peach season. Of course you could use yellow varieties, but somehow those childhood memories of tinned peaches with yellow vanilla ice cream and jelly come wobbling back.

In my experience, white peaches are usually of the 'Clingstone' variety – i.e. the flesh clings to the stone. The neatest way to remove the flesh is not to cut around the peeled peach and twist it, but peel the peach and then slice off the flesh either side of the stone, as you would a mango, and then slice off the rest as neatly as possible.

750ml bottle Frascati, or similar lively fruity white wine
110g sugar
1 vanilla pod, split lengthways
3 cardamom pods, split to reveal seeds
20cm cinnamon stick
$^1/_2$ tsp fennel seeds
3 strips orange peel, pith removed
700g peaches
400g raspberries

Mix half of the wine with the sugar in a non-reactive pan and dissolve, stirring, over a low heat. Add the vanilla, spices and orange peel. Bring to the boil and simmer for 20 minutes. If the syrup is thickening, add a little more water to prevent it from turning to caramel. Take the pan off the heat and add the remaining wine. Leave to cool.

Bring a large pan of water to the boil and put in the peaches. Leave for about 30 seconds and certainly no longer than one minute before straining the peaches and plunging them into cold water. Using a sharp knife, lift the blanched skin off the fruit and neatly slice the fruit off from the stone. Cut into bite-sized pieces and place in a bowl. Strain the wine spice syrup over the peaches through a sieve. Mix gently with the raspberries. Refrigerate and eat the same day. Serve in pretty glasses.

serves 6

peppered balsamic strawberry and mascarpone tart

Balsamic vinegar and black pepper elevate ripe strawberries to greatness. Here the rich tang of the berries melds beautifully with the cool mellow mascarpone cream and the crisp light pastry. Finally, the glistening reduced syrupy juices give this luxurious summer dessert a sharp peppery kick.

You will need a loose-based 26cm flan tin.

for the balsamic strawberries
750g ripe strawberries, hulled
$1^1/_2$ tbsp good balsamic vinegar
2 tbsp caster sugar
1 level tsp pink peppercorns, finely ground
several twists of black pepper

for the sweet pastry case
180g plain flour
90g salted butter, chilled
2 large egg yolks
1 tbsp icing sugar

for the mascarpone filling
350g mascarpone
250ml double cream
50g caster sugar
3 tsp lemon juice

for the balsamic strawberries

Place the strawberries in a bowl and sprinkle with the vinegar and caster sugar. Toss them gently. Sprinkle over the pink pepper and twist over a generous seasoning of black pepper. Cover and refrigerate for around 2–4 hours (too long and the fruit will become mushy and dull).

for the sweet pastry case

Place the flour and butter in a food processor and pulse until like breadcrumbs. Pour into a bowl and add the yolks and icing sugar. Bring the mix together with your fingertips. Put in a plastic bag and leave in the fridge for at least 2 hours. Remove the pastry from the fridge at least 20 minutes before using. Preheat the oven to 180C/350F/Gas4. Roll out the pastry to 3–4mm thick and ease it into the flan tin. Patch the pastry as necessary with off-cuts and fold excess pastry from around the edges back into the tin, pressing it against the side, leaving a raised edge. You will be trimming this pastry after around 10 minutes of baking. This method leaves a very neat edge to the tart. Line the pastry with a disc of baking paper and fill with baking beans. Bake for 10–12 minutes, or until the pastry edge is becoming firm and a touch golden. Remove the case from the oven and, using a serrated knife, trim the pastry to the level of the top of the tin. Remove the baking beans and baking paper, prick the base a few times with a fork, and bake for a further 5 minutes, or until the pastry base is golden and crisp.

to assemble the tart

Combine the mascarpone filling ingredients. Whip well to aerate the mixture.

Strain the strawberries through a colander, retaining the juice in a small non-reactive pan. Be careful not to damage the fruit through over-handling. Reduce the juices to a syrup over a moderate heat for around 5 minutes. Leave to cool.

Place the cooled tart case on a serving plate. Spoon in the mascarpone mixture and level it with a spatula. Slice the strawberries in half lengthways and arrange them over the cream. You don't have to be too artistic. It will look fantastic however you arrange them.

Serve as soon as possible with a drizzle of the kicking peppery tangy strawberry reduction.

serves 8–10

black pepper

The West's favourite flavour enhancer; this is the spice that really got the likes of Vasco de Gama and Marco Polo heading East. With its pungent, earthy, fruity, rich, yet clean and biting flavour, pepper must be held responsible for centuries of death and destruction at sea and on land across Asia and Europe. It was incredibly valuable. The quaint term 'peppercorn rent', which these days refers to a piffling outlay originally meant quite the opposite.

Pepper berries grow on vines on dangling stems, and when still green are harvested, fermented and dried. The black colour seems to be produced as a result of interacting with a parasite fungus. Nice. Though pepper is exported from many countries, the best quality pepper undoubtedly comes from its original homeland, India. The vastly superior Indian Malabar or Indian Tellicherry berries are left on the vine longer than many of the others, which means that the piney smoky taste contained in the pepper oil enjoys more time to develop.

Whatever you do, do not buy ground pepper. Enjoy the best flavour and save your money by buying whole 'corns from an internet site (see *shopping for spices*, page 125) or an Asian supermarket. Grind them yourself in a pepper grinder, pestle and mortar or in your spice grinder.

poached pears with spiced syrup and toasted almond cream

The mild aromatic flavour of poached pears make them great candidates for gentle spicing. Here they are poached in a light spice syrup and stuffed with a rich toasted almond cream. You can leave out the stuffing if you like, but I feel that the hole in the poached pear where the core once was is aching to be filled.

Don't use Conference pears – they tend to fall over and although they have a great flavour, they are too slim for stuffing. Prepare this dessert at least a few hours in advance to allow the pears to chill thoroughly and for the syrup spices to infuse.

You'll have syrup left over. Keep it in the fridge; it's great with anything from ice cream to steamed puddings.

You will need a pan that will neatly accommodate the six pears, preferably upright.

for the pears
540g sugar
700ml water
6 fairly ripe medium pears (e.g. Williams, Rocha)
20cm cinnamon stick
1 vanilla pod, split lengthways
5 slices peeled fresh ginger root
2 strips lemon rind, pith removed
4 pieces star anise
8 cardamom pods, split to reveal seeds
3 cloves
juice of one lemon
generous pinch salt

for the toasted almond cream
1 large egg yolk
30g sugar
2 tsp plain flour
2 tsp cornflour
1 vanilla pod (or $1/4$ tsp vanilla extract)
200ml milk
100ml double cream
30g ground almonds

to poach the pears

Place the sugar in the pear pan and pour over the water. Set on a low heat to dissolve the sugar, stirring from time to time. Meanwhile, prepare the pears. Peel off the skin from stem end to base in long confident strips to give a pleasing neat result. Most recipes suggest to core the pears at this point, but I core them post-poaching – the pear is softer and so it's easier.

Once the sugar has dissolved, bring the syrup to the boil and simmer for one minute. Add the cinnamon, vanilla, ginger and lemon rind. Place the pears in the syrup and weight them down with a small plate. (If the syrup doesn't cover the pears totally, you will have to turn them after 10 minutes poaching.) Simmer gently for a total of 20–30 minutes. The poaching time will depend on size and ripeness of the fruit. When cooked, a small sharp knife will sink easily through the flesh down to the core. Turn off the heat and leave the pears to cool in the syrup for 20 minutes or so before removing them from the syrup to cool, covered, in the fridge.

to complete the spiced syrup

To the syrup, add the star anise, cardamom, cloves, lemon juice and salt. Bring to the boil and simmer for a minute or two. Take off the heat and leave to stand for at least an hour and a half. If not using straight away, strain the syrup to prevent it from becoming too pungent. Keep the spices though, as a couple of scraps from this beautiful debris look great on the finished dish.

to make the toasted almond cream

Beat up the egg yolk with the sugar in a roomy bowl until pale and creamy. Add the flour and cornflour and combine well. Split the vanilla pod, if using, and scrape out the seeds.

Pour the milk into a saucepan and whisk in the vanilla seeds or extract. Bring the milk to the boil and pour directly onto the egg mix, stirring. Return the mixture to the pan and stir over a low heat to thicken, which it will do alarmingly quickly. Just keep stirring and any lumps will sort themselves out. Cook for around 5 minutes, stirring all the time, to 'cook out' the flours. Take off the heat and beat in the double cream.

Heat the grill to moderate. Spread the ground almonds over an oven tray and place under the grill to toast. Stir the almonds around once they start to take colour. Watch very carefully as they will turn from perfectly golden to useless acrid brown in seconds. Allow to cool before beating them into the cream.

to complete the dish

Core the pears making a generous hole into which you will pipe or spoon the almond cream. Fill the pears with the cream. Stand each pear upright on a plate. Just before serving, spoon plenty of syrup over and decorate the plate with spices from the syrup.

serves 6

late summer pavlova with cinnamon meringue and spiced plums

Pavlova, the classic antipodean dessert, is one of my summer favourites. When the berries are past their best, look no further than plums to carry the spirit of the recipe through into autumn. The tartness of the spiced plums cuts the sweet cinnamon meringue and cream perfectly.

for the meringue
6 egg whites
375g caster sugar
$1^1/_2$ tbsp cornflour
3 tsp white wine vinegar
1 heaped tsp freshly-ground cinnamon

for the spiced plums
$1^1/_2$kg ripe red plums, halved and destoned
5 tbsp water
50g unrefined brown sugar
$1^1/_2$ tsp freshly-ground cinnamon
3–4 large sprigs rosemary

to finish
approximately 500ml whipping cream
2 tbsp toasted pine nuts (optional)

for the meringue

Preheat the oven to 150C/300F/Gas2.
Line your largest oven tray with baking paper.

Place the egg whites in a squeaky clean bowl and beat them with an electric whisk until they form stiff peaks. Be very careful not to over-beat the whites giving a grainy and separated appearance; this will cause the finished meringue to collapse. Add one tablespoon of the sugar to the egg white. Beat well before adding the next and the next and so on until all of the sugar is used up. Add the cornflour, vinegar and cinnamon and beat for a further few minutes. You will have a sturdy glossy speckled meringue.

Pile the meringue onto your lined oven tray and, using a spatula, spread it out into an attractive 'nest'. Bake the meringue for around $1^1/_2$ hours, or when a skewer inserted into the heart of the meringue comes out clean. The meringue may well take a little colour. If becoming too dark, lower the oven temperature to 140C/275F/Gas1.

for the plums

Preheat the oven to 190C/375F/Gas5.

Place the plums, cut side up, in a ceramic oven dish, or on a paper-lined lipped metal tray. Sprinkle over the water. Mix the sugar with the cinnamon and spoon directly over each plum. Tuck the rosemary in between the plums. Place the tray in the oven and cook for around 20–40 minutes or until the fruit has darkened and softened, and is giving up some juice as syrup. The cooking time will vary largely depending on the size and ripeness of the fruit. If the plums are taking too much colour before softening, cover them with foil. Once cooked, remove from the oven and allow to cool.

to assemble

Whip up the cream to soft peaks. Spread over the meringue. Top with the cooled plums and juices. Serve scattered with the toasted pine nuts, if using.

serves 8–10

stone fruit doughnut fritters with cinnamon sugar

What I love about this pudding is that each anonymous crisp golden sugar-crusted two bite-size fritter holds its own bright tangy spicy mystery fruit. Red, yellow, green, orange, purple, you never know what you're going to get next. Select beautifully ripe but firm fruit. A couple of peaches, a few red plums, a couple of apricots and a handful of greengages offer a spectacular variety of colour and flavour. With the added cool crunch of cinnamon sugar, this makes the most delicious and entertaining summer pudding. Serve the fritters simply as they are, or with cream for dipping.

280g strong white flour
1 tbsp caster sugar
$1/4$ tsp salt
1 x 7g sachet dried yeast (or 20g fresh yeast)
200ml cider
160ml water
450g stone fruit
100g caster sugar
3 tsp freshly-ground cinnamon
a few tbsp of flour for tossing
oil for frying (ground nut is best)

to prepare the batter

Put the flour, one tablespoon of sugar, salt, yeast, cider and water in the bowl of a mixer fitted with either a dough hook or a K-beater. Beat for 5–7 minutes, or until a smooth shiny batter. Alternatively, it's quite therapeutic to slap the dough around a bowl with your hand for 5 minutes. Cover the bowl with Clingfilm and leave in a warm place for an hour or so to prove, or until it has bubbled throughout and has approximately doubled in size.

to prepare the fruit

While the batter is proving, prepare the fruit. Wash and cut each piece of fruit into largish one-bite-size chunks, de-stoning as you go. Mix the 100g of sugar with the cinnamon. Place the chopped fruit in a bowl or plastic container and toss with just one heaped tablespoon of the cinnamon sugar. Leave to one side until you are ready to fry the fritters.

to make the fritters

Beat the batter back with a wooden spoon. It should be like runny dough. You are now ready to fry the fritters. Have ready a tray lined with a few layers of kitchen paper and a slotted spoon or 'spider'. Set the oil to heat up to around 170–180C/335–355F. Use either a calibrated deep-fat fryer, or a sugar thermometer in a deep pan of oil. If you have neither, test the oil after 5 minutes of heating with a small dollop of batter; it should begin to brown after a minute or so. Spoon the flour onto a plate or metal tray and toss on four pieces of cinnamon sugar-coated fruit. Make sure the fruit pieces have a light coating of flour before transferring them one at a time to the batter. Using a dessertspoon, turn a piece of fruit in the batter and making sure it is enveloped in the batter, spoon it into the hot oil. Repeat with the remaining three pieces of fruit. Turn the fritters in the oil to ensure even browning. The fritters will take around 3 minutes to cook. Using the slotted spoon, remove them to the kitchen paper to drain. As you become more adept at coating the fruit with batter, increase the number of fritters you are frying at one time.

to serve

Arrange the fritters on a serving plate and scatter with the remaining cinnamon sugar. Serve as soon as you can with cream for dipping.

**makes 30–40 fritters
(enough for 5–6 people)**

tarte reine-claude, lightly spiced

Greengages look and sound pretty unpromising. A green stone fruit must surely be sour, hard and underripe. Not at all. They are great as they are, make memorable jam and are terrific in pies and cakes.

Known by the French, more romantically as 'reine-claude', the greengage was introduced to France, probably from Asia Minor, during the 16th century reign of Francois 1. This delicious fruit, invariably sweet as honey and tart at the same time was named in honour of Claude, the king's good and popular Queen Consort.

This tart demonstrates what an impact a subtle sprinkling of freshly-ground spices can make on the whole character of a fruit pudding. Here I use lively spices to complement the zing of the fruit.

You will need a 26cm loose-based flan tin.

one quantity sweet pastry (see *peppered balsamic strawberry and mascarpone tart*, page 12)
450g greengages
1 tbsp eau de vie or schnapps
2 large eggs
180ml whipping cream
120g caster sugar
$^{1}/_{4}$ tsp freshly-ground star anise
$^{1}/_{2}$ tsp ground ginger
1 tbsp flour
1 tbsp soft brown sugar for sprinkling

Roll out the pastry to 3–4mm thick and ease it into the flan tin. Fold excess pastry from around the edges back into the tin, pressing it against the side, leaving a raised edge. Roll the rolling pin over the top of the tin to leave a neat edge. Place the tart case in the refrigerator for at least one hour before using.

Wash, dry and quarter the greengages, removing the stones. You'll need a small pointed knife, as the stones can be clingy. Place the prepared fruit in a bowl and toss with the alcohol. Leave aside for one hour before using.

Place a baking tray in the oven and preheat it to 190C/375F/Gas5. This preheated tray will help to accelerate the cooking of the pastry base. Place the eggs in a bowl and break them up with a fork. Reserve a scant tablespoon of the beaten egg in a cup to use for brushing the pastry later. Add the cream to the beaten eggs and combine well. Add the caster sugar, spices and flour and beat, using a whisk if necessary, until smooth. Strain the juice from the marinating greengages and mix into the batter.

Take the pastry case out of the fridge and brush with the reserved egg. Arrange the fruit over the base. Pour over the batter. Sprinkle over the soft brown sugar. Bake for 30–40 minutes, or until the top of the tart is well browned and the pastry is crisp.

Leave to cool. Eat the same day.

serves 8

buttery glazed pear & vanilla tart

Pear and vanilla make great partners. They both have a rounded, mellow, blousy flavour, which tunes in well with the sweet-bitterness of caramel. In this stunning golden vanilla-flecked tart, the smooth flavours and textures of the ingredients sit in a crisp buttery crust. I find that pears are a touch flabby and vacuous when hot or even just warm. I prefer this tart at room temperature, when it sets slightly and is transformed into the best of patisserie.

You will need a 26cm loose-based flan tin.

for the pastry
180g plain flour
90g salted butter, chilled
2 large egg yolks
1 level tbsp icing sugar

for the filling
1kg firm just-ripe pears
55g salted butter
65g vanilla sugar (or caster sugar if not available)
1 vanilla pod, split lengthways
3 tsp lemon juice
2 tbsp Poire William, eau de vie or schnapps

for brushing
egg white

to make the pastry

Place the flour and butter in a food processor and pulse until like breadcrumbs. Pour into a bowl and add the yolks and icing sugar. Bring the mix together with your fingertips. Put in a plastic bag and leave in the fridge for at least 2 hours.

Remove the pastry from the fridge at least 20 minutes before using. Preheat the oven to 180C/350F/Gas4. Roll out the pastry to around 3–4mm thick and ease it into the flan tin. This pastry is pretty unruly and you may need to patch it up a bit with off-cuts. Fold excess pastry from around the edges back into the tin, pressing it against the side, leaving a raised edge. Roll the rolling pin over the top of the tin to leave a neat edge. If not using straight away, keep it in the fridge.

to prepare the pears

Quarter the pears lengthways, peel and core them. Slice into $1^1/_2$cm thick wedges. Put the cut pear into a non-reactive pan with the butter, vanilla sugar, the split vanilla pod, lemon juice and alcohol. Cook on a low heat, barely simmering, until softened, but definitely not collapsing; about 8–10 minutes depending on ripeness. Strain the pears through a colander, retaining the buttery juices and transfer to a large plate to cool rapidly; you don't want the fruit to cook any further. Remove the split vanilla pod.

to make the tart

Place a baking tray in the oven and preheat it to 190C/375F/Gas5. This preheated tray will help to accelerate the cooking of the pastry base. Brush the pastry case with egg white. Fill the tart case with the pear. Place the tart on the oven tray and bake for 25–30 minutes, or until both the pastry and pears are browned. If you find that the pastry is taking too much colour, reduce the oven temperature to 180C/350F/Gas4.

While the tart is cooking, place the buttery juices from the pears in a small non-reactive pan and reduce them to a caramel of about half the original volume. Place the vanilla pod on a plate and using the rounded point of a table knife, strip out the tiny seeds. Being careful not to lose any, whisk the seeds into the reduced caramel.

When the tart is baked, remove it from the oven and pour over the caramel. Reduce the oven temperature to 180C/350F/Gas4 and return the tart to the oven for 5 minutes. Ideally, leave the tart to cool and serve it at room temperature. If you prefer to eat it warm, leave the tart to cool for at least 15 minutes before serving, as the pastry tends to collapse any earlier.

serves 8

vanilla

Don't use vanilla essence. It is not vanilla at all and has a harsh one-dimensional flavour and a bitter aftertaste. The aroma imparted from vanilla pods is full and creamy, blousy and rich with a complex aroma, sometimes a touch smoky with a suggestion of dried figs. Either on its own, or in combination with other spices, vanilla gives a beautifully rounded flavour to a dish.

Vanilla is, however, very expensive. I hate to throw a vanilla pod away. If you have used it in a fat-free recipe, such as a syrup, rinse the pod and keep it for another occasion. There's always some flavour left. I would urge you to keep any unused vanilla pods packed in sugar, providing you with delightful and very versatile vanilla sugar.

The fresh vanilla pod, as harvested from an exotic climbing orchid, is virtually scentless. The high cost of vanilla stems from a lengthy fermenting and drying process, which takes several weeks. If you find vanilla pods coated with a white powder, do not overlook them; this is the best vanilla you can buy. The coating or 'givre' is a frosting of pure vanillin crystals.

intense rhubarb and ginger caramel

This rich little dessert conveys the very
essence of rhubarb, packing a powerful
rhubarb punch, which is pronounced even
further by the fresh ginger and lemon zest.
Serve it simply as it is, or possibly with a light
crisp biscuit such as *light spice sablé biscuits*
(page 88).

When choosing your rhubarb, try to pick out
pink stems. You can use frozen rhubarb, which
tastes fine and for some reason tends to yield
a nice coloured result.

You will need six 9cm ramekins.

butter for buttering the ramekins
for the caramel
75ml water
160g sugar
for the rhubarb mixture
450g rhubarb
2 tsp finely grated peeled fresh ginger root
zest of 1 lemon
220g sugar
45g salted butter, room temperature
3 tsp plain flour
4 large eggs, beaten

Lightly butter the ramekins.

to make the caramel

Place the water and sugar in a non-reactive
pan. Have ready a bowl of iced water large
enough to accommodate the pan. Place the pan
on a low heat and stirring, allow the sugar to
dissolve. Once dissolved, bring the syrup to a
simmer. Do not stir from this point, but watch
the caramelisation process carefully. When the
syrup is a rich amber colour, plunge the pan
into the cold water to arrest the caramelisation
and remove again swiftly to prevent
hardening.

Spoon a dessertspoon of caramel into each of
6 ramekins.

to make the pudding

Preheat the oven to 170C/325F/Gas3.

Chop the rhubarb into 3cm long pieces and
put into a non-reactive pan with the ginger,
lemon zest and sugar. Cook until the rhubarb
is soft, around 15 minutes.

Allow the rhubarb mixture to cool for 20
minutes before beating in the butter, flour
and beaten eggs. Pour into the 6 ramekins
and stand in a deep oven tray. Pour water into
the tray up to the level of the mixture in the
ramekins. Place in the oven and bake for
25 minutes or until firm to the touch.
Do not allow them to soufflé; they will split.

Allow to cool for 15 minutes before running a
knife round them and turning them out with
great ease onto plates.

serves 6

mango and five spice tarte tatin

The original and best upside-down pudding, here the tarte tatin is turned into a shining caramelised dessert, rich in colour and flavour. The butteriness of the ripe mango blends beautifully with the buttery caramel of the tart. This richness is cut with lime and given an aromatic edge by the five spice. This spice blend is usually used for savoury dishes, but is actually a very sweet concoction (see *chinese five spice powder*, page 26), which makes a magical and exotic marriage with mango. In baking the tarte tatin, mangoes give out more juice than the traditional apple. The addition of the cornflour helps to set this juice into the tart.

which mango?

Mangoes come in all sizes. Sweetness, fibrousness and intensity of flavour can vary enormously. I love the small Pakistani or Indian mangoes you find in independent Asian stores. Though sometimes unpromisingly dull on the outside, inside they are sweet and tart, buttery and vibrant in colour and flavour. Perfect for the following recipe. Supermarkets tend to drum out the immaculate, but relatively bland-flavoured large green and red varieties. Whatever you use, be sure to use ripe fruit.

You will need a 24cm cake tin.

1kg ripe mangoes
1 heaped tsp Chinese five spice (see page 26)
1 tbsp icing sugar
3 tsp cornflour
zest and juice of 1 lime
100g salted butter
50g soft brown sugar
50g white sugar
300g puff pastry

Preheat the oven to 180C/350F/Gas4. Line the cake tin with a 35cm diameter piece of baking paper. This larger piece of baking paper will hold the bubbling juices as the tart cooks.

to prepare the mango flesh

To obtain as much undamaged mango flesh as possible, don't skin the flesh until it is sliced. So, using a sharp knife, slice the mango flesh from either side of its flat stone. Cut each side into 2cm thick pieces, rather like chunky potato wedges. To skin, place each piece skin side down on the chopping board and holding the knife flat to the board, run it along just inside the skin, as if skinning a fish fillet. Cut the remaining ring of skin from around the stone and slice off any residual flesh into as large wedges as possible. Place the mango pieces in a roomy bowl.

to make the tart

In a small bowl, mix the five spice, icing sugar and cornflour. Add this mixture to the mangoes and toss. Sprinkle with the lime zest and juice.

Place the butter and sugars in a small frying pan over a medium heat. Bubble up and allow to cook gently, keeping stirring to a minimum, for 7–8 minutes, or until the mixture darkens slightly, curdles and then re-amalgamates into thick 'ropes'. If the mixture stays curdled, don't worry, there is margin for error here.

Just don't let the mixture darken too much. Roll out the pastry to a thickness of around 4–5 mm. Place the prepared cake tin on the pastry and cut a circle of pastry out $1^1/_2$cm greater in radius than the tin. Remove the paper-lined tin from the pastry and carefully pour in the still hot caramel. Arrange the mango pieces over the caramel. You don't have to be too careful about this; the mango pieces slip into place nicely and it'll look great whatever you do. Scrape over any remains from the mango bowl. Place the pastry over the mango and, trying to prevent any juices or caramel from flooding over the pastry, lift and tuck the pastry edge carefully down around the mango.

Bake the up-side-down tart for 25–30 minutes, until the pastry is well risen and browned. Allow to cool for a good 25 minutes before removing the tart from the tin cradled in its baking paper, invert onto a plate. Marvel at its beauty and serve as is, or with Greek yoghurt.

serves 6

chinese five spice powder

You can buy it, but it's so much more fun to make your own. To me using a bought spice mix feels like buying a cake mix. When you whiz up your own spice blends, the flavours are cleaner, and you can guarantee freshness.

The basic five of five spice are star anise, fennel seeds, cinnamon, cloves and Szechwan pepper. Some use liquorice root instead of the star anise, black pepper can substitute for Szechwan pepper and some contain ginger. Here's my favourite version. I know; it contains six spices.

2–3 star anise
1 tsp Szechwan peppercorns
5cm cinnamon stick
$^1/_2$ tsp fennel
$^1/_4$ tsp ground ginger
2 cloves

Grind to powder in a spice grinder.

makes 4 teaspoonfuls

grilled pineapple with vodka and cracked black pepper

This simple yet explosive tasting pud is plucked from the book *Blistering Barbecues*, the sizzling recipe dossier of the al fresco catering company of the same name. Barbecue chefs know only too well that by the time you've cooked off your burgers and the rest, you won't want to be turning out anything too complicated. But if you think ahead and marinade the pineapple before your guests arrive, the rest is easy.

Pineapple is the king of barbecue fruits. Try to get hold of the 'Supersweet' variety. They are almost as good as the sensational ripe fruit you commonly buy in, for example, India or Thailand. And pepper is as named; it peps the flavour up even higher. Serve warm with whipped cream.

1 large ripe pineapple
6 tbsp vodka
1 tsp cracked black pepper, or several twists from a grinder
300ml whipping cream, whipped

to prepare the pineapple

Cut off the top and bottom of the pineapple and place on a chopping board, flat bottom downwards. Using a large serrated-edged knife cut off the skin in long strips, from top to bottom, and work round the pineapple until all the skin is removed. The flesh will be studded with eyes of deeply imbedded skin. Cut these out with the point of a sharp kitchen knife. Slice the pineapple into quarters down through the hard core and then slice out the core. Transfer the quarters to a plate and splash over the vodka. Sprinkle over the pepper. Cover and refrigerate for at least an hour, or overnight is fine.

You'll need a hot barbecue. Brush your racks clean of any debris and oil the bars lightly with a cloth. Grill the pineapple quarters for 4–5 minutes, or until charring and caramelised.

Transfer the grilled pineapple to a chopping board and slice into two-bite-size chunks. Transfer to a serving plate, pouring over any vodka marinade that was left behind, and spike each piece with a bamboo skewer. Serve warm with whipped cream for dipping.

serves 6

compotes, moulds, creams and custards

What better than something tangy, spicy and fruity, whether warm or chilled, checked by a cool and creamy foil.

light coconut nutmeg blancmange with fresh mangoes in a spiced syrup
panna cotta with any spiced fruit compote
spiced gooseberry crème brûlée
caramelised bramleys with thick whipped cream
spiced plum compote with cinnamon toast and greek yoghurt
fresh apricot compote with sweetened fromage blanc
east indian creamy cardamom rice with hunza apricots in spiced jaggery
   syrup
spiced cherry sablé
sharp and spiced berry compote
small dried fruits in spice syrup

light coconut nutmeg blancmange with fresh mangoes in a spiced syrup

This light refreshing coconut blancmange is a revelation. Coconut and nutmeg visit similar spots on your palate and complement each other beautifully. If you can get reduced-fat coconut milk do so. The blancmange is even lighter.

The tongue-tingling mango preparation is the perfect exotic partner for the creamy coconut blancmange. Make the most of the spices and leave the fruit to soak overnight. You could also try the mangoes with *clove and maple syrup ice cream* (page 51) or *east indian creamy cardamom rice* (page 38).

Choose the best mangoes (see page 24).

You will need six 9cm ramekins or darioles for the blancmanges and a piece of muslin and some string to bag up the spices for the mango.

for the blancmange
300ml coconut milk (full or reduced-fat)
75ml milk
150g caster sugar
$1/4$ tsp freshly-grated nutmeg
zest of 1 lime
2 tsp powdered gelatine
200ml whipping cream

for the mangoes in syrup
3 tbsp sugar
4 tbsp water
10cm cinnamon stick
1 tsp coriander seeds
2 pieces star anise
generous pinch chilli flakes
3 cloves
juice of 1 lime
pinch salt
1 tbsp maple syrup
1kg mangoes

to make the blancmange

Put the coconut milk with the milk, sugar, nutmeg and lime zest in a pan. Heat gently until the sugar has dissolved. When at almost 'ouch' finger hot, take off the heat and sprinkle the gelatine over the liquid. Stir until dissolved (about 3 minutes). Leave to cool and refrigerate. When beginning to set, whip up the cream and fold it into the coconut mix.

Sprinkle the ramekins or darioles with water, tapping out any excess. Divide the mixture between the moulds and return, covered, to the fridge. They will take a few hours to set properly and are fine overnight.

to make mangoes in spiced syrup

Place the sugar and water in a non-reactive pan. Allow the sugar to dissolve over a low heat before the syrup simmers. While the sugar is dissolving, lightly bash the spices with a pestle and mortar, just to break them up a little. Tie the bruised spices up in a piece of muslin with a bit of string.

Once the sugar has dissolved, add the spice bag, lime juice and salt. Simmer for five minutes before taking off the heat and adding the maple syrup. Leave to stand for at least 30 minutes for the spice flavours to infuse into the syrup. I'd leave it longer, but it's up to you to decide on the potency of the spice in the syrup.

Cut the mango into 1cm thick slices. (See 'to prepare the mango flesh', page 24). Place the prepared mango into a serving dish and cover with the syrup. Leave the muslin bag of spices in the syrup for as long as you like. Refrigerate and leave to steep overnight.

to serve

Loosen the blancmanges from their moulds by gently pushing down round the edge with your finger. Upturn the individual blancmanges onto dessert plates and surround with mango. Dribble over the syrup.

serves 6

nutmeg

Nutmeg is my comfort spice. Relatively gentle, it is warm and sweet, slightly clovey, but with a dangerous edge of camphor. Ground nutmeg begins to lose its aroma rapidly the moment you grate it. So grate it directly into any recipe requiring it. For me, nutmeg is inseparable from sweetened egg dishes, from clafoutis (page 73) to eggnog (page 108) via custard tart (page 83).

Nutmeg is one of the spices that make up the sweet Dutch spice mix, Speculaas (see *cox apple streusel cake with speculaas*, page 66). In their colonial days, the Dutch protected their nutmeg crops on the Spice Islands vigorously, burning down warehouses of spices to increase the value of their crops and doing everything they could to prevent the spice from being grown anywhere else. The local wildlife was their undoing; birds carried the seeds to neighbouring islands and the consequent inexorable spread of saplings proved beyond their control.

Hanging on a tree in the Spice Islands, a nutmeg resembles an apricot. Peel back the flesh to reveal the brilliant fleshy red skin of mace wrapped around the dark shell encasing the nutmeg. The mace is removed and the nutmegs are left to dry in their shells. After a month or two rattling around inside, the kernel or nutmeg is ready. The thin shells are cracked and the nutmegs are revealed. Uncomplicated and nobbly; you can grate the whole lot.

You may have heard of the hallucinogenic properties of nutmeg. The spice's oil does indeed contain a mescalin-related hallucinogen, myristicin. You would have to eat a lot of nutmeg to have any effect, so I'd take those apocryphal Women's Institute nutmeg biscuit stories with a pinch of salt. However, those Malaysians who ate any number of a particular once-popular sweetmeat of whole nutmegs boiled in syrup may have been in a spot more of bother.

panna cotta with any spiced fruit compote

This trembling dessert presents a perfect creamy backdrop for tangy, spiced fruit compotes. The trick with panna cotta is to obtain a sort of almost-sinking wobble. Too much gelatine and you may as well buy a supermarket blancmange. If a panna cotta could express itself as it was turned out of its mould, it would sigh with a 'flurp'.

Serve with a spiced fruit compote – *fresh apricot* (page 37), *sharp and spiced berry* (page 42) or with *oranges preserved in brandy and spiced syrup* (page 116).

You will need six 9cm ramekins.

600ml double cream
1 vanilla pod, split lengthways
finely pared rind of 1 lemon, pith removed
75ml milk
2 level tsp powdered gelatine
50g icing sugar
60ml grappa, eau de vie or schnapps

Put about three quarters of the cream into a small pan with the split vanilla and lemon rind. Gently bring to the boil. Simmer for 2–3 minutes and take off the heat. Leave to stand for 20 minutes to infuse the flavours.

Heat the milk to 'ouch' finger hot and sprinkle in the gelatine. Stir to dissolve. Whisk the remaining cream with the icing sugar and alcohol until just slightly thickened.

Strain the milk-gelatine mix through a sieve into the warm vanilla cream and mix well. Combine with the whipped sweetened cream. Decant the mixture into the ramekins and transfer to the fridge. Leave to set for at least 4 hours. Overnight is good, but make sure they are tightly covered.

To serve, loosen the panna cottas from their ramekins by gently pushing around the edge with your finger. Upturn them onto dessert plates and surround with spoonfuls of spiced fruits.

makes 6

spiced gooseberry crème brûlée

Hot and cold. Sugar and spice. Sweet and sour. Heaven on earth.

I've always felt that the best crème brûlée is chilled at the bottom and hot at the top. So start this pudding the day before and have all the little cream pots lined up ready in the fridge for a last minute caramelisation under a super-hot grill, just as you are ready to eat them.

I've used vanilla extract (not essence) here. I didn't want the expense and extra palaver of vanilla pods deterring you from trying this delicious dessert.

You will need six 9cm ramekins.

450g gooseberries, washed, topped and tailed
4 tbsp water
40g stem ginger, finely chopped
1$\frac{1}{2}$ tsp freshly-ground cinnamon
4 whole cloves
90g brown sugar
4 tbsp water
4 large egg yolks
25g caster sugar
550ml double cream
few drops of good vanilla extract
2 tbsp caster sugar
1 heaped tsp ground ginger

for the spiced gooseberries

Place the prepared gooseberries in a non-reactive pan with the water, ginger, cinnamon, cloves and brown sugar. Cook over a gentle heat for 5 minutes or until the berries soften. Stir regularly to prevent sticking and squash them with the back of the spoon to accelerate the process. Take off the heat and leave the cloves to infuse while you make the custard.

Preheat the oven to 140C/275F/Gas1.

for the egg custard

Beat the egg yolks with the 25g of caster sugar in the bowl of a double boiler, or in a bowl that fits snugly over one of your pans. In another pan, heat the cream and add the vanilla extract. Pour the hot cream onto the egg mixture and stir. Place above the simmering water and cook, stirring regularly until the custard coats the back of a spoon.

to make the crème brûlée

Pass the gooseberries through a sieve, pushing with the back of a tablespoon, to remove the cloves and tough skins and pips. Divide the resulting purée between the ramekins. Carefully strain the custard over the gooseberries making sure that the gooseberries don't mix with the custard.

You will be baking the crème brûlée in a bain marie. Place the ramekins into a tray containing 2cm water. Bake in the oven for around 30 minutes, or until they are just set. Leave to cool and refrigerate, covered, for at least 4 hours; preferably overnight.

to finish

Preheat the grill to high.

Mix the 2 tablespoons of caster sugar with the ground ginger and sprinkle it evenly over the brûlée. Run your finger around the inside of the ramekin above the brûlée to clean off any clinging sugar. Using the bain marie tray, fill with 2cm of iced water and place the ramekins in the water. Place under the grill and watch like a hawk as the sugar melts and browns. Remove and serve after a few minutes, when the top will have set hard.

serves 6

caramelised bramleys
with thick whipped cream

Tart, intense and throaty, this simple little dessert swings me straight back to the apple room in my childhood home, where my Mum neatly laid out on newspaper all the ripe fruit from our garden in the late summer. I could still smell the apples in there when it was eventually turned into a spare bedroom.
This was one of the delicious puddings that she baked on autumn evenings. We had it with Bird's custard, as could you, but nowadays I prefer it with whipped double cream.

You could use coxes, but they don't quite have the same tang and creamy texture.

You will need six 9cm ramekins or a single pudding bowl or brioche tin.

butter for buttering the mould/s
for the caramel
100ml water
175g sugar
for the apples
$1^1/_2$kg Bramley apples
100g brown sugar
$^3/_4$ tsp freshly-ground cinnamon
1 level tsp ground ginger
150ml water
3 large eggs, lightly forked
to serve
300ml double cream, whipped

Butter the ramekins, pudding bowl or brioche tin.

to make the caramel

Place the water and sugar in a non-reactive pan. Have ready a bowl of iced water large enough to accommodate the pan. Place the pan on a low heat and stirring, allow the sugar to dissolve. Once dissolved, bring the syrup to a simmer. Do not stir from this point, but watch the caramelisation process carefully. When the syrup has passed through amber and is darkening further, plunge the pan into the cold water to arrest the caramelisation and remove again swiftly to prevent hardening. Pour the caramel into your chosen mould/s and swill it around the sides a little too.

to make the caramelised apples

Preheat the oven to 180C/350F/Gas4.

Peel, core and slice the apples into 2cm chunks. Place in a pan with the sugar, spices and water. Cook over a moderate heat for 15–20 minutes, or until the apples are soft. Some will be mushy, some still intact. Allow to cool to just warm before beating in the eggs. Divide the mixture between the moulds.

Cook in a bain marie. That is, place the filled moulds in a deep baking tray and pour hand-hot water into the tray up to the level of the apple mixture. Bake ramekins for 15–20 minutes and a pudding bowl or brioche tin for 25–30 minutes.

Serve warm, chilled or at room temperature inverted onto plates or a plate and served with whipped double cream.

serves 6

spiced plum compote with cinnamon toast and greek yoghurt

Plum and spice make a great late summer partnership. But teamed with hot cinnamon toast and cool Greek yoghurt, you've got all the great contrasts. Not only do you have sugar and spice, but also hot and cold, crunchy and smooth and mellow and tart.

Cinnamon toast is a forgotten luxury. Hot, dripping, light, soft-yet-crunchy, caramelised, doughnutty, golden... eat it with hot chocolate, coffee, cream, ice cream, bacon, as well as fruit compotes... it's utterly delicious and very very simple to make... as long as you watch the grill closely. Butter switches from golden and caramelised to burnt and bitter in seconds. Use thick bread and plenty of good salty butter.

You'll find other delicious plum spice combinations in the *yoghurt plum cake with pecans and spices* (page 70) and in the *late summer pavlova with cinnamon meringue and spiced plums* (page 16). If I have any leftover bits of second-hand vanilla pod, I throw these into the spice mix too.

You will need a piece of muslin and some string to bag up the spices.

for the compote
30cm cinnamon stick
4 cardamom pods, crushed
3 cloves
225ml red wine
150g soft brown sugar
750g ripe red plums

for the cinnamon toast
6 x 2cm thick slices good fresh white bread
salty butter
1$^1/_2$ tbsp sugar
1$^1/_2$ tsp freshly-ground cinnamon

to finish
500g of Greek yoghurt

to make the compote

Lightly pound the cinnamon, cardamom and cloves in a pestle and mortar, just to loosen them up a bit, and tie them up in a piece of muslin with a bit of string. Put the wine and sugar into a non-reactive pan and place over a moderate heat. Allow the sugar to dissolve slowly before the pan simmers, at which point you add the spice bag.

Wash and slice the plums into halves and remove the stones. Add them to the simmering spiced wine mixture and cook gently for 15 minutes or so, or until the plums are soft. Take off the heat and leave to cool.

to make the cinnamon toast

Preheat the grill to moderate.

Toast the bread lightly on both sides. Butter very generously. Slice the crusts off neatly. In a small bowl, mix the sugar with the cinnamon. Sprinkle this over the buttered toast and transfer to the grill. Watch very carefully as the sugar melts and the edges brown. There may be a little light smoke from the caramelisation before you achieve cinnamon toast perfection, but hold your nerve – 2–3 minutes should do it. Serve immediately with a few spoonfuls of compote and a generous dollop of Greek yoghurt.

serves 6

cinnamon

Cinnamon has been around for millennia, cropping up a number of times in the Bible; if not amongst other treasures such as myrrh, gold and frankincense, it's being used to perfume beds. It's even found in Sanskrit texts, so there's been plenty of time for unscrupulous merchants to find ways of ripping you off. If you care about spice quality, cinnamon shopping is a minefield. The best comes from Sri Lanka and it comes in three forms: sticks or quills, ready-ground, or bark.

To understand the varying qualities of cinnamon, you need to understand how it's harvested. The outer bark is stripped off to reveal the inner, paler, finer bark; the substance of cinnamon sticks. The outer bark is sold as 'bark' and looks like bark too. The delicate inner bark is scored long ways and then taken off in quills; a skill undoubtedly passed on from father to son. The quills are dried in the shade and then rolled with great dexterity into sticks, any stray broken bits being packed into the stick once formed. Take a stick apart and you'll see how it's made.

Forget ready-ground; once the lid's off, the flavour's on the wane. And what's more, you don't know what you're getting – all the stray off-cuts, chippings and bits of bark from the floor can be chucked into the grinder. Buy sticks from a reputable dealer, and the paler the better. Sticks have a sweet and warm, pungent, rounded, full and blousy aroma with a subtle edge of citrus. Bark still has a terrific cinnamon odour, but is more one-dimensional, tighter, harsher, and yes, woodier. If you're boiling cinnamon in syrup or mulling with other spices, the cheaper bark will do fine. Otherwise use sticks for sweet dishes and keep the bark for savoury spice mixes. Stock up in Asian stores, but beware of the shady merchant who is passing off shaped bark as sticks. Some of the bark may even be cassia, a close relative of cinnamon with an uglier more pungent and less pleasing aroma. I told you it was a minefield.

fresh apricot compote
with sweetened fromage blanc

For me, this is France. A few spoonfuls of the sunniest compote of them all, vibrant in colour and tang, alongside a small mound of fromage blanc, sprinkled with crunchy white sugar.

Use ripe apricots for the best taste and colour.

Try substituting peaches and grappa.

You will need a piece of muslin and some string to bag up the spices.

600g ripe apricots
75g sugar
100ml water
10cm cinnamon stick
4 cloves
1 tbsp Amaretto
500g fromage blanc
1 tbsp coarse granulated sugar

Halve or quarter the apricots (depending on size) and discard the stones.

Place the sugar and water in a non-reactive pan. Allow the sugar to dissolve over a low heat before the syrup simmers. While the sugar is dissolving, lightly bash the cinnamon and cloves with a pestle and mortar, just to break them up a little. Tie the bruised spices up in a piece of muslin with a bit of string.

Once the sugar has dissolved, add the spice bag and Amaretto along with the prepared apricots. Stir to make sure the fruit is evenly covered with the syrup and place over the low heat again to bring slowly to a simmer. Cover and simmer very gently for 8–12 minutes. Check from time to time that the apricots are cooking evenly and that they are not breaking up too much. Note that the fruit will continue to cook as it cools. Serve at room temperature with a spoonful of fromage blanc sprinkled with sugar.

serves 6

east indian creamy cardamom rice with hunza apricots in spiced jaggery syrup

This rice is a classic sweet and cleansing pudding. Every small restaurant from Delhi to Calcutta has some version of this dessert lurking in the back of its fridge. You may choose to set the rice in individual bowls or ramekins, as is traditional (usually in stainless steel cups). Alternatively, prepare the rice in one large bowl, spoon some of the nut-strewn rice onto a dessert plate and serve with the Hunza apricots. Try substituting the apricots for *small dried fruits in spiced syrup* (page 43).

When cooked, dried Hunza apricots have an incredible rich toffee flavour. Dried, they look pretty uninviting; the colour of peanut shells and the appearance of knobbly nutmegs. But don't let any of this put you off. The best ones come from Afghanistan where they are dried in the sun. If you are lucky, as I am, to live near to a fantastic and imaginative grocer, you can buy fresh Hunza apricots for a five-week (or so) season from around the end of August.

You will need six 9cm ramekins, small gratin dishes, or similar. Or use one small serving bowl if not making individual puddings.

for the cardamom rice
6 green cardamom pods
30g salted butter
35g basmati rice
1 bay leaf
2 litres whole milk
100g sugar
75g sultanas
2 level tbsp pistachio nuts, almonds and
  pine nuts, toasted and chopped

for the Hunza apricots
30 dried Hunza apricots
2 large strips lemon zest
50g jaggery, or rough brown sugar
15cm cinnamon stick
water to cover plus 2cm

to make the cardamom rice

Using a sharp knife, split open the cardamom pods and prize out the little black seeds. Pound the seeds in a pestle and mortar until fine. Melt the butter in a large stainless steel heavy-bottomed pan. Add the rice and cook for a couple of minutes until the grains just begin to pick up a nutty hue. Add the bay leaf and the milk. Bring to a boil, reduce the temperature and simmer, stirring from time to time, until the volume is reduced by half (about 30 minutes). Add the sugar, sultanas and cardamom. Continue to simmer, stirring more assiduously to prevent sticking, until the volume is reduced by roughly half again (about 20 minutes), or until the milk becomes thick and creamy and is massing nicely with the rice. Note that the rice will continue to set as it cools.

Remove from the heat and spoon into the serving bowl/s. Sprinkle with the chopped nuts, cool and refrigerate for at least 3 hours before serving.

to make the apricot compote

Put all ingredients in a small non-reactive pan and bring to a simmer. Simmer gently, covered, for 20 minutes. If drying out, add more water. Allow to cool. Remove the strips of lemon zest and cinnamon stick before serving with the chilled cardamom rice.

serves 6

spiced cherry sablé

Here's a dessert striking both on the eye and palate. Crisp biscuit, cool yoghurt and zingy spiced cherries combine to make a stunning end to a summer supper. Or try with *sharp and spiced berry compote* (page 42).

Like plums and apples, cherries are one of those tart, but rich-flavoured fruits that have broad enough shoulders to carry some confident spicing. If you can't get hold of sour cherries, use a firm dessert variety. This compote is also delicious as an alternative to the plums in the *late summer pavlova* (page 16) or with *panna cotta* (page 31).

Don't embark on this recipe unless you have a cherry stoner. You will also need a piece of muslin and some string to bag up the spices.

for the cherry compote (approximately 500ml)
750g sour cherries
3 tbsp sugar
3 tbsp brandy
3 tbsp water
10cm cinnamon stick
2 cloves
3 strips finely pared lemon rind
2 tsp lemon juice
2 level tsp arrowroot

to finish
400g Greek yoghurt
18 *light spice sablé biscuits* – i.e. one recipe
   quantity (page 88)
1 tsp freshly- and finely-ground cinnamon
1 heaped tbsp icing sugar

to make the compote

Stone the cherries using a cherry stoner (that may seem obvious, but if you use any other method, the finished cherry compote will not look great).

Place the sugar with the brandy and water in a non-reactive pan. Allow the sugar to dissolve over a low heat before the syrup simmers. While the sugar is dissolving, lightly bash the cinnamon, cloves and lemon rind with a pestle and mortar, just to break them up a little. Tie the bruised flavourings up in a piece of muslin with a bit of string. Once the sugar has dissolved, add the spice bag and lemon juice along with the prepared cherries. Place over the low heat again to bring slowly to a simmer. Cover and simmer very gently for 8–10 minutes. The cherries should soften, but not lose their shape. Take the pan off the heat.

In a small cup, mix the arrowroot with a couple of teaspoonfuls of water and stir into the cherry compote, making sure it is well distributed. Leave to cool.

to assemble the dessert

Line up six dessert plates. Place a scant teaspoonful of yoghurt on each plate and pop a biscuit on top. The small amount of yoghurt will stop this biscuit from sliding around. Top with a heaped dessertspoonful of the yoghurt. Repeat on all six plates. This should use up half of the yoghurt. Spoon the cooked cherries over the yoghurt, using half of the cherries between the six plates. You will find that some of the cherries will stick to the yoghurt and others will roll around. Don't worry; this is part of the charm. Place a second biscuit over the yoghurt and cherries at a jaunty angle. Spoon the rest of the yoghurt over the second biscuit and top with the rest of the cherries. Place the final biscuit on the top. Spoon the cherry juices around the plates.

Combine the cinnamon with the icing sugar in a small bowl and sieve or scatter over the dessert for a great finishing touch.

serves 6

sharp and spiced berry compote

This jewel-bright compote makes the perfect accompaniment to *panna cotta* (page 31). The sharpness of the berries picks up on the citrussy edge of cinnamon, but is otherwise softened by the cushion of spice flavours and rounded off beautifully with the vanilla. You may wish to add a little more sugar, but I prefer it as it is. Your choice of berries will affect the tartness of the finished compote. My favourite combination would be along the lines of 150g raspberries, 150g blackberries, 120g blackcurrants and 80g redcurrants. If using redcurrants, avoid excessive tartness by not exceeding this quantity. In any case, do not use strawberries; they become flabby on cooking.

You will need a piece of muslin and some string to bag up the spices.

3 tbsp sugar
4 tbsp water
2 tsp balsamic vinegar
10cm cinnamon stick
1 piece star anise
1 bay leaf
1 vanilla pod, split lengthways
500g mixed berries (see the favoured mix above)

Put the sugar in a small non-reactive pan with the water and vinegar and place over a low heat. Allow the sugar to dissolve before the syrup simmers. While the sugar is dissolving, lightly bash the cinnamon, star anise and bay leaf with a pestle and mortar, just to break it all up a little. The spices will not be in the syrup for long, so best to increase their surface areas by breaking them down. Tie the bruised spices up in a piece of muslin tied with a bit of string.

Once the sugar has dissolved, add the bag of spices and the split vanilla pod and bring to a simmer. Simmer for a few minutes. Now add the berries. Add any firm skin berries such as redcurrants, blackcurrant, bilberries or blueberries first and let them simmer for no more than $1^1/_2$ minutes. Then add the other softer berries such as raspberries, blackberries and loganberries and stir gently into the syrup. Cook for 30 seconds or so and take off the heat. Leave to cool. Test the syrup for spice flavour as it cools and remove the bag when you feel the time is right. Also remove the vanilla pod and put it on a plate. Using the rounded point of a table knife, strip out the tiny seeds. Decant a spoonful of the syrup from the berries and mix the vanilla seeds into it, making sure they are well broken up. Return the vanilla syrup to the pan.

Leave to cool and serve at room temperature.

makes about 500ml

small dried fruits in spice syrup

I've never really liked the larger pieces of fruit in a mixed-dried or 'winter' fruit salad. Rather like an over-sized oyster, the texture of a mouthful of cooked dried prune or fig is just too challenging. And there's never enough syrup either. So here's my dream compote featuring all the smaller fruits and lots of syrup.

There is a baffling range of sultanas and raisins, which come in all shades from green to black through red and yellow. There are the most delicious large yellow-green sultanas from Iran and Afghanistan and equally large juicy yellow sultanas from Australia. Fat and black, Muscatel raisins come from all over Europe and the sensational Lexia raisin; dark red and long as your fingertip are generally available around Christmas. You can get hold of dried cranberries, cherries and even blueberries if you hunt around. You could always add chopped apricots too. If you make sure you have plenty of the delicious paler sultanas and of the dried berries, the resulting compote can be as colourful as a pack of Jelly Beans.

It's traditional to soak the dried fruit overnight in tea rather than water, but quite frankly, with all the fruity flavours going on, I simply cannot taste the difference. I like this compote as it is, but you could head off in two further separate directions. Either make a richer concoction by adding brandy, calvados or some such spirit to the soaking liquid, or simply finish the dish with a splash of rosewater to produce a more fragrant compote. Don't use both.

Serve it with *east indian creamy cardamom rice* (page 38), or *cinnamon toast with greek yoghurt* (p35).

for soaking
200g dried fruits (sultanas, raisins, dried cherries, dried cranberries, dried blueberries, chopped dried apricots)
20g (about one level tbsp) finely chopped stem ginger
15cm cinnamon stick
2 cloves
water to cover completely plus 2cm
2 tbsp brandy, calvados or rum (optional)
to cook
150ml apple juice
150ml water
80g brown sugar
splash of rosewater to taste (optional)

Place the dried fruit, stem ginger and spices in a bowl and pour over water and spirit if using. Leave to soak overnight.

Tip the entire contents of the bowl into a stainless steel pan and add the apple juice, water and sugar. Bring to a simmer and cook for around 20 minutes, or until the fruit has softened. Leave to cool. If using, add rosewater to taste.

makes 500ml

spiced ice

There's nothing really linking this collection of luxurious ices together, except that is for temperature. Whether clove and maple syrup ice cream is melting seductively over steaming apple pie, or mango lime and chilli sorbet is refreshing your exhausted taste buds after a fiery Indian feast, or if you are presenting flaming festive alaskas to your Christmas guests, there are plenty of opportunities to mix spice with ice.

gooseberry and ginger yoghurt ice
mango, lime and chilli sorbet
saffron and cardamom ice cream
cinnamon toffee ripple ice cream
clove and maple syrup ice cream
flaming festive alaskas
christmas pudding and rum sauce ice cream

gooseberry and ginger yoghurt ice

Like rhubarb, gooseberries have a great affinity for ginger. And there's no cloying cream here throwing a blanket over the zing; the lightness of the yoghurt allows the starry flavour of the gooseberries and fresh ginger to shine through. This ice would be as light and fruity as a sorbet but for the starchy consistency of cooked gooseberries, which makes for a more substantial texture.

You could use ground ginger or stem ginger syrup, but fresh ginger is another creature all together, making for a cleaner pepperiness, which sets off the gooseberries beautifully. If you were to add fresh ginger directly, you'd split the yoghurt. Making a ginger syrup, as described below, gets round this problem.

250g sugar
140ml water
100g finely chopped peeled fresh ginger root
500g gooseberries, washed and halved
  lengthways
250g Greek yoghurt

Place the sugar and water in a small pan. Heat gently to dissolve the sugar. Once dissolved, simmer the syrup for one minute. Add the chopped ginger and continue to simmer gently for 5 minutes. Take off the heat and allow the ginger to steep in the syrup for 10 minutes. You can leave it for longer, but you could end up with an overpoweringly gingery finished ice. Taste the syrup and make up your own mind, bearing in mind that the freezing dulls the strength of flavour.

Place the gooseberries in a pan. Strain the ginger syrup through a sieve into the pan, squeezing the last drops out of the ginger with the back of a spoon. Cook the gooseberries over a gentle heat for about 5 minutes or so, or until softened. Allow to cool slightly before transferring to a blender. Whiz the contents and strain through a coarse sieve or chinois to remove tough skin and pips. Chill the purée in the fridge. Stir in the yoghurt.

If you have an ice cream machine, switch on the stirrer and pour in the gooseberry mixture. Once frozen, transfer to a clean container in the freezer. If you don't have an ice cream machine, transfer the mix to a clean plastic container and place in the freezer to set. Stir the mixture at 2-hour intervals over a period of 6 hours. If frozen solid, take out of the freezer half an hour before serving.

makes approximately 800ml

mango, lime and chilli sorbet

Just as it does with savoury dishes, in desserts chilli stimulates the palate and turns up the volume of flavour. Here, in harmony with the sharp zing of lime, the chilli picks up the intense buttery flavour of mango and prettily flecks the bright yellow ice with vivid red.

The rich dense texture of mango brings a luscious smoothness to sorbet. Catch the short, but golden, Indian mango season in April and May, or the Pakistani season which follows, and you will find the best fruit in the world; the king of all fruits. Serve as a double-iced dessert with *saffron and cardamom ice cream* (page 49).

1 large red chilli, or to taste
225g sugar
325ml water
650g ripe mango flesh (from approximately
  1kg mangoes)
zest of 2 limes
juice of 3 limes

It is important to the appearance, flavour and texture of this sorbet that the chilli be very finely chopped. To finely dice the chilli, you would be well advised to don a pair of rubber gloves. Using a sharp knife, halve the chilli lengthways. Chop off the stem end and the very tip and flatten one half of the chilli. Remove the seeds and the line of pith with the flat of the knife. Cut the chilli lengthways into very thin (1–2mm wide) strips. Gather these together and again using a sharp knife, chop into tiny dice. Repeat with the other half of the chilli.

Place the sugar and water in a small pan. Heat gently to dissolve the sugar. Once dissolved, simmer the syrup for one minute. Take off the heat and add the chopped chilli. Leave to cool for 20 minutes.

Prepare the mango flesh and place in a blender. Strain the syrup through a sieve into the blender, retaining the chilli. Whiz until smooth. Pass the mango purée through a coarse sieve or chinois into a bowl and add the lime zest and juice. Return the chopped chilli to the mixture. Chill in the fridge.

If you have an ice cream machine, switch on the stirrer and pour the sorbet mixture in and once frozen, transfer to a clean container in the freezer. If you don't have one, transfer the mix to a clean plastic container and place in the freezer to set. Stir the mixture at 2-hour intervals for 6 hours. If frozen solid, take out of the freezer half an hour before serving.

makes 1 litre

fresh ginger root

When used fresh in recipes, ginger root has a clean, sharp taste contrasting with that of dried ground powder, which may be hotter, but contributes a more rounded, almost dusty and toasted flavour to recipes. Fresh ginger is straight to the fiery, citrusy, peppery point. The two flavourings are not really interchangeable.

This is yet another of those spices which you should buy in Asian supermarkets. The turnover there is great, so you're more certain to get hold of fresh firm juicy ginger rhizomes. It will also be cheaper.

To prepare ginger in syrup, otherwise known as 'stem ginger', the root is peeled and cut into chunks before simmering repeatedly in sugar syrup. Stem ginger is a terrific ingredient adding flavour and texture to biscuits (*world's best ginger biscuits*, page 90) and cakes and puddings (*spiced dessert cakes and tarts*, pages 65–83).

saffron and cardamom ice cream

Here the traditional 'kulfi' is turned into a richer classic ice cream. Saffron and cardamom are two of the most expensive hand picked spices available, so this is a pretty luxurious concoction. It can be served on its own, with an appropriate compote such as *hunza apricot* (page 38), or dropped into a glass of refreshing *mango lassi with jaggery, ginger and cardamom* (page 106).

To obtain the cardamom seeds, cut open the pods and scrape out the little black seeds from the three inner chambers.

1 large pinch saffron
200ml milk
seeds from 12 cardamom pods
$1^1/_2$ tsp freshly-ground cinnamon
225g sugar
6 large egg yolks, blended
400g yoghurt
200ml double cream, whipped

Infuse the saffron for 10 minutes in 2 tbsp hot water. Pour the milk into a non-reactive pan. Crush the cardamom seeds in a pestle and mortar and add to the pan with the saffron and its water and the cinnamon. Bring to the boil. Take off the heat and leave to infuse for at least one hour.

In the bowl of a double boiler, blend the sugar with the egg yolks. Strain the milk over this mixture and combine all together with a wooden spoon. Place the bowl over a pan of simmering water and cook, stirring, for 20 minutes or so, or until the spiced custard coats the back of a spoon. Take off the heat and allow to cool. Once cool, mix in the yoghurt and fold in the whipped cream. Chill well.

If you have an ice cream machine, switch on the stirrer and pour the ice cream mixture in and once frozen, transfer to a clean container in the freezer. If you don't have an ice cream machine, transfer the mix to a clean plastic container and place in the freezer to set. Stir the mixture at 2-hour intervals over a period of 6 hours. If frozen solid, take out of the freezer half an hour before serving.

makes approximately 1 litre

cinnamon toffee ripple ice cream

During my ice cream tasting sessions, this one was ubiquitously adored. Even by a one-year-old. The combination of cinnamon and caramel pops up all over this book and here it is in a very simple form. By happy coincidence, this is also the easiest ice cream of all to put together. It makes a terrific accompaniment to virtually any cake or pudding in this book.

350g toffees
175ml milk
3 tsp freshly-ground cinnamon
550ml whipping cream

Place the toffees, milk and cinnamon in a pan over a low heat and allow the toffee to melt, stirring from time to time. Once melted, transfer to a plastic container and leave to cool. Whip the cream to soft peaks. Stir about two-thirds of the cooled toffee mixture into the cream, holding back the other third to fold in later to make the 'ripples'.

If you have an ice cream machine, switch on the stirrer and pour the ice cream mixture in. Once the ice cream has reached the consistency of a heavy béchamel sauce, scrape it quickly into a clean plastic container and fold in the remaining toffee mixture, leaving visible ripples. Transfer to the freezer.

If you don't have an ice cream machine, transfer the ice cream mixture to a clean plastic container and place in the freezer to set. Stir the mixture at 2-hour intervals over a period of 6 hours. Fold in the remaining toffee mixture on your last stir to create toffee ripples through the mixture.

If frozen solid, take out of the freezer half an hour before serving.

makes 1 litre

clove and maple syrup ice cream

Delicately clovey and warm with maple syrup, this ice cream is tailor-made to accompany autumn fruit puddings such as the *caramelised bramleys* (page 34), *cox apple streusel cake* (page 66) or *rhubarb and ginger caramel steamed pudding* (page 59). Place the open clove jar next to the open maple syrup bottle and put one nostril over each. You'll see what a happy marriage they make.

You should note that any flavour is dulled by freezing. The clove may seem too prominent in this ice cream's pre-frozen state, but in fact, the following clove quantity, coupled with the steeping time, makes for a delicate flavour in the finished ice. If the ice cream is being made to accompany a heavily spiced pudding, you may wish to increase the clove quantity, or steep it for longer.

400ml milk
15 cloves
50g sugar
6 large egg yolks
4–5 tbsp maple syrup
350ml double cream

Put the milk and cloves into a pan and heat to boiling. Take off the heat and leave the cloves to steep in the milk for about 45 minutes. Strain through a sieve.

In the bowl of a double boiler blend the sugar with the egg yolks. Pour the milk over this mixture and combine all together with a wooden spoon. Place the bowl over a pan of simmering water and cook, stirring for 20 minutes or so, or until the spiced custard coats the back of a spoon. Take off the heat and allow to cool, stirring from time to time. Mix in the maple syrup. Whip the cream until it reaches soft peaks and fold into the clove mixture. Chill in the fridge.

If you have an ice cream machine, switch on the stirrer and pour the ice cream mixture in, and once frozen, transfer to a clean container in the freezer. If you don't have an ice cream machine, transfer the mix to a clean plastic container and place in the freezer to set. Stir the mixture at 2-hour intervals over a period of 6 hours. If frozen solid, take out of the freezer half an hour before serving.

makes approximately 1 litre

flaming festive alaskas

This Christmas, skip the heavy pudding, brandy butter and the rest, and wow the jaded family with a flaming Alaska. It has all the taste of Christmas, but is lighter and miles more exciting.

And there is no work on the day. This heavenly meringue-covered ice cream and cake confection is whisked directly from the freezer into the oven and is ready in five minutes. Turn down the lights and carry two at a time flaming to the table.

You could make one big one for a fantastic impact, but I prefer the texture of the ice cream in individual ones.

8 flat slices cake, Madeira, Victoria, ginger or
   carrot – whatever you have in the cake tin
8 large scoops (one recipe quantity) *christmas pudding and rum sauce ice cream* (page 54)
4 medium egg whites
225g caster sugar
pinch salt
8 small sprigs holly
half a ladle rum or brandy for flaming

Cut out eight square slices of cake measuring 6–7cm wide and $1^1/_2$–2cm thick. Alternatively stamp out circles of cake of the same thickness measuring 7–8cm in diameter. Find a tray or trays that will fit into your freezer and line them with baking paper. Place the cake slices on the trays leaving at least 5cm between each slice. Top each slice with a large ball of the ice cream. This should be around the size of a small apple or approximately 80g. Place the trays in the freezer and leave for at least 1 hour before topping with the meringue.

Leave at least 30 minutes before starting the meringue. Place the egg whites, caster sugar and salt in the bowl of an electric mixer and beat until smooth and white, but still thin (about 1 minute). Place the mixer bowl over a pan containing a few centimetres of simmering water and whisk until the meringue mix is hot (about 2–3 minutes). Test the temperature with your finger. Your mix is hot enough when it just reaches 'ouch' temperature. Remove the bowl from the pan and return it to the mixer. Beat until the meringue is stiff and shiny (about 3–4 minutes). Allow to cool to room temperature before spreading over the ice cream.

You could use an icing bag with a star-shaped nozzle for a retro look, but I prefer to spread the meringue over the ice cream with a knife dipped in hot water. Then rough it up with the tip of the knife. Whatever you do, be sure to cover the ice cream completely to the depth of at least 1cm. Either bake them immediately or return the meringue-covered Alaskas to the freezer until they are needed.

To bake, preheat the oven to 220C/425F/Gas7. Take the Alaskas straight from the freezer to the oven and bake for 4–6 minutes, or until the meringue has taken a good colour. Remove from the oven and insert a holly sprig into each pudding. You're not racing against the clock here. Your natural instinct may be telling you that the ice cream is melting away, but you'll find that the cake and meringue act as very effective insulating blankets.

To flame, you need a helper. Men love a little flame action, so select one from your party. If you have a gas hob, have him heat the rum or brandy in the ladle over the gas and ignite it with a match. If electric, just use a pan. Lower the lights and pour a little flaming alcohol over two of the puds and take them to the table. Oooooooooh! Carry on until they are all cooing like turtle doves.

serves 8

christmas pudding and rum sauce ice cream

Ice cream is a bit like soup. Once you've got the hang of the techniques, it's a delicious way to use up tasty leftovers and borderline over-ripe fruit. Christmas pudding is a virtually guaranteed leftover. And it's a testament to how concentrated its flavour is how little you need to make an ice cream which fills you with the memories of Christmas. Serve with *cinnamon toast* (page 35), as a duo with *clove and maple syrup ice cream* (page 51) or in a cornet with a sparkler on New Year's Eve.

50g sugar
500ml milk
4 large egg yolks
2 tbsp rum
175g raw or cooked Christmas pudding
75ml whipping cream

First make the rum sauce. Put the sugar with the milk in a pan and heat it to boiling. Meanwhile, beat the egg yolks in the bowl of a double boiler. Pour the hot milk over the yolks, stirring as you do so. Place the bowl over simmering water and cook the sauce gently for around 20 minutes, or until it is thick enough to coat the back of a spoon. Add the rum.

If the Christmas pudding is not cooked, place it in a microwave-proof bowl covered with Clingfilm. Cook in the microwave on full power for 3 minutes, or until soft. Allow to cool 10 minutes before blending with a ladle of the rum sauce in a food processor, or using an electric wand blender. Mix the runny pudding mix with the rum sauce. Refrigerate until well chilled. Whip the cream to soft peaks and fold into the chilled mix.

If you have an ice cream machine, switch on the stirrer and pour the mixture in, and once frozen, transfer to a clean container in the freezer. If you don't have an ice cream machine, transfer the mix to a clean plastic container and place in the freezer to set. Stir the mixture at 2-hour intervals over a period of 6 hours. If frozen solid, take out of the freezer half an hour before serving.

makes about 600ml

spiced indulgence

No fresh fruit here. Just stickiness, caramel, chocolate and booze. Cul-de-sacs of indulgence.

syrupy spiced babas
rhubarb and ginger caramel steamed pudding
soft-centred dark chocolate ginger and orange puddings
sweet and sticky medjool date pudding-cake with middle eastern spices
prune and armagnac soufflé
kouign amann (breton butter cake) with cinnamon

syrupy spiced babas

From Greece, through Armenia to Iran, from
Azerbaijan to the tip of Saudi you find the most
beautiful syrup-drenched pastries packed with
dried apricots, dates, almonds and pistachios and
scented with cardamom, cinnamon, rose water
and saffron. I'll leave the intricacies of baklavas
and other glistening delicacies to the experts, but
here's my own tribute to the genre; light yeast
pastries soaked with plenty of spiced syrup and
scattered with chopped pistachios. Yes, I know
babas originated in Poland, but they are the
perfect vehicles to absorb and purvey the
aromas of the Souk.

You can get hold of the dried rose petals in
Middle Eastern stores. Dried yeast is used here,
because it's easier to get hold of than fresh
yeast, and I want to leave no impediment to
anyone tempted to try this heavenly recipe.

You will need a 12-cup muffin tray.

for the syrup
400g sugar
520ml water
10 cardamom pods, lightly crushed
30cm cinnamon stick
2 tsp coriander seeds, lightly crushed
8 strips lemon rind
6 strips orange rind
$1/4$ tsp salt
1 tbsp dried rose petals
juice of $1/2$ lemon

for the babas
150g plain flour
1 x 7g sachet dried yeast (or 20g fresh yeast)
20g caster sugar
finely grated zest of 1 lemon
80g sultanas
3 egg yolks
110ml warm milk
75g salted butter, melted
butter for greasing the muffin tray
3 tbsp pistachios, chopped, for sprinkling

to make the syrup

Put the sugar and water into a non-reactive
pan. Place over a low heat and stir until the
sugar dissolves. Add the spices, lemon and
orange rinds and salt and bring to the boil.
Simmer gently for 5 minutes. Take off the
heat and add the dried rose petals and the
lemon juice. Leave the spices to steep while
you prepare the babas.

to make the babas

Mix the flour with the dried yeast, sugar,
lemon zest and sultanas in a warmed bowl.
Make a well in the centre and add the yolks.
Mix a few tablespoons of the milk with the
yolks before adding the rest of the milk and
the melted butter. Mix everything together
with a spoon and beat it well. The consistency
should be closer to a batter than a dough, but
lies somewhere between the two. Cover with a
damp cloth and leave in a warm place for
30–45 minutes until doubled in size.

Beat the dough back. Grease the 12-cup muffin
tray lightly with butter. Divide the dough between
the cups. Cover again with a damp cloth and
leave to rest and rise for 15 minutes. Meanwhile,
preheat the oven to 180C/350F/Gas4.

Bake for 15–20 minutes, or until cooked through.
Transfer the cooked babas directly to a lipped
tray or plate that accommodates them neatly.
Prick them mercilessly with a cocktail stick
and spoon over the syrup while the babas are
warm. They must be soaked through, so carry
on spooning the excess syrup over them from
time to time for the next half hour.

Once cool, sprinkle with the chopped nuts.
The pastries keep very well in or out of the
fridge. Serve as they are with mint tea, or if
you want to cut your life expectancy, with a
dollop of thick cream.

makes 12 babas

chillies

Chillies are a major appetite stimulant and will lift any flavour. In Thailand, they accompany anything from sea slugs to mango. I deal with mango elsewhere (*mango in spiced syrup*, page 29) and dabble in other fruits (*tropical fruit salad with chilli*, page 9), but in *mr greenwood's cha cha cha chillies* (page 102) I mix chilli with chocolate. If it's good enough for the Mexicans....

Why is chilli so addictive? Pleasure is realised through pain. Natural opiates released in the brain to dull the burn remain well after the chilli heat has subsided, leaving you sitting on a cushion of pleasure. Or maybe eating chillies is like white water rafting, exhilarating and scary at the same time, leaving a sense of euphoria afterwards. Whatever the explanation, its original discovery way way back in South America must have transformed the lives of those used to eating bland roots and staples.

Capsaicin, the natural chemical responsible for the 'heat' in chillies has been found to be made up of several components, each of which dances or stamps out its own tune on a different part of your tongue and mouth. The balance of these natural chemicals in each chilli is responsible for the differing aggressiveness and background flavours in each variety. Most of the chilli's capsaicin is stored in the white pith of the fruit, so if you want to reduce the heat, remove as much of the pith as you can.

rhubarb and ginger caramel steamed pudding

Squashy, homely and delicious. To me this represents everything that is best about a steamed pudding; it is moist, syrupy, spicy and inseparable from thick custard.

You will need a 500g pudding bowl and one recipe quantity of cooled *gingery calvados caramel sauce* (page 123).

butter for buttering the pudding bowl.
200g rhubarb
3 tbsp water
2 heaped tbsp sugar
1 level tsp ground ginger
125g salted butter, room temperature
125g caster sugar
2 large eggs
125g self-raising flour
40g stem ginger, finely chopped
1 recipe *gingery calvados caramel sauce* (page 123), cooled

Butter the pudding bowl.

Slice the rhubarb into $1^1/_2$cm pieces and place in a pan with the water, the 2 tablespoons of sugar and the ground ginger. Cook over a moderate heat, stirring to prevent sticking. Add a little more water if the rhubarb is drying out before it softens. Leave to cool.

To make the pudding batter, beat the butter with the 125g of sugar until pale and light. Add the eggs one at a time with one tablespoon of the flour to prevent 'curdling'. Add the rest of the flour and the stem ginger. Pour the cooled rhubarb (just warm is fine) over the mix and fold twice. The finished pudding should have ripples of the rhubarb running through, so do not mix any more than this.

Spoon four tablespoons of the Calvados caramel sauce into the base of the pudding bowl. Scrape the rhubarb batter mix into the bowl. It may swim rather in the caramel sauce, but this is how it is meant to be. Tie a piece of buttered foil over the bowl with a single pleat to accommodate the growing pudding. Place the bowl in a pan of gently simmering water for $1^1/_2$ hours. The water should go no further than three-quarters of the way up the sides of the bowl.

Taking great care, remove the bowl from the hot water and dry it with a towel. Remove the foil and turn the pudding out onto a deep-rimmed plate.

Serve with the rest of the caramel sauce, and some thick custard.

serves 6

soft-centred dark chocolate ginger and orange puddings

I would not usually contaminate chocolate with other flavours. But with a small handful of spices, including ginger, cinnamon (*hot cinnamon chocolate with cream*, page 111) and chilli (*cha cha cha chillies*, page 102), I would make an exception. Ginger makes chocolate even more dusky, dark and dangerous.

This pudding, adapted from my pastry chef days, is simply delicious – and as spectacular as it is easy. I'm at a loss to suggest what to serve it with, maybe a beautiful vanilla ice cream. But I just serve it on its own with a shake of icing sugar. The cooking time is the key to this weepingly lovely dessert. Don't be tempted to go over the prescribed time, and serve it immediately.

You can make the mixture ahead, storing the filled moulds covered in the fridge. Remove them from the fridge 30 minutes before baking.

You will need eight moulds; either 9cm ramekins, or best of all, metal darioles.

butter and flour for lining the moulds
150g darkest cocoa-packed chocolate
150g salted butter
4 freshest eggs
2 freshest egg yolks
75g caster sugar
1 level tbsp plain flour
fine zest of 1 large orange
either 1 heaped tsp ground ginger
or $1/2$ tsp ground ginger and 25g stem ginger,
  finely chopped

The ramekins or darioles need to be buttered and floured thoroughly. Any gaps and the pudding will stick. After buttering the moulds, place a tablespoon of flour into one of them and tap around all of the surface right up to the rim, making sure that it covers every bit of butter. Tip the excess flour into the next mould and do the same, carrying on until all six moulds are coated.

Preheat a baking tray in the oven to 220C/425F/Gas7. If the filled moulds are placed on oven-hot trays, the base of the pudding will cook more quickly.

Melt the chocolate with the butter in a bowl over a pan of just-below-simmering water. Be careful not to overheat the mixture, as the chocolate will spoil. Slip a wooden spoon in between the bowl and the pan to allow steam to escape.

Meanwhile beat the eggs and yolks up with the sugar, using an electric whisk, until pale and thickened. Once the chocolate and butter are melted, stir them together and pour them into the egg mixture with the flour, orange zest, ground ginger, and stem ginger if using. Stir gently, folding everything together until totally combined. Divide the mixture between the moulds. Transfer directly to the hot trays in the oven. Cooking is swift; 5–7 minutes if using metal moulds; more like 8–9 minutes if using Pyrex or ceramic.

Remove from the oven and allow to cool for a couple of minutes. Run the point of a sharp knife around the outside of the pudding and invert it onto a plate. The pudding will slip out easily. Serve within 10 minutes.

serves 8

sweet and sticky medjool date pudding-cake with middle eastern spices

Make room for this one. You could use ordinary dates, but Medjool dates are the largest, sweetest softest dates on the market. Great on their own and terrific in this heavenly sticky dessert. Here we are making a single cake, but you could make individual puddings and adjust the cooking time appropriately.

There are a couple of optional spices in the ingredients list. Only optional, because they may be tricky to get hold of. This is the thing with spices; none of them are strictly necessary to a recipe, but each spice you add changes its character. Saffron and sumac do add an extra Middle Eastern charm.

Delicious with *oranges preserved in brandy and spiced syrup* (page 116), or *apricot sauce* (page 124) and a swirl of cream or Greek yoghurt.

You will need a 20cm loose-based cake tin.

butter for lining the tin
175g Medjool dates, stoned
275ml water
pinch saffron (optional)
1 tsp freshly-ground sumac (optional)
1 tsp freshly-ground cinnamon
seeds from 5 cardamom pods, finely crushed
1 tbsp rose water
50g salted butter, room temperature
150g caster sugar
2 large eggs
150g self-raising flour
1 tsp bicarbonate of soda

Preheat the oven to 180C/350F/Gas4. Butter and line the cake tin.

Place the stoned dates in a pan with the water. Bring to the boil and simmer until the interiors of the dates begin to break down. Turn off the heat and add the spices and rose water. Leave to cool.

Beat the butter with the caster sugar in an electric mixer for 4–5 minutes, or until good and pale. Add the eggs one at a time, beating between additions to make sure both eggs are perfectly incorporated.

Blend the date and spice mixture either in a food processor, or with a wand mixer. You don't want to melt the butter, so wait until the date mixture is close to cool before adding it to the butter mixture. Sieve in the flour and bicarbonate of soda and fold in. Pour the runny batter into the prepared tin.

Bake for around 50 minutes to one hour, or until a skewer comes out of the cake clean. If the surface of the cake is becoming too dark, turn the heat down to 170C/325F/Gas3 until the cake is cooked through.

Serve warm or at room temperature, and as suggested above.

serves 8

prune and armagnac soufflé

Break open this indulgent soft-centred soufflé minutes after it leaves the oven to release a cloud of Armagnac and spices. Pour in chilled cream, or chilled *spiced plum sauce* (page 124) and enjoy the rich toffee flavour of prunes mingling with cinnamon and ginger.

You will need eight 9cm ramekins.

butter and caster sugar to line the ramekins
130g dried stoned prunes
60ml apple juice
1 tsp ground ginger
1 tsp freshly-ground cinnamon
2 tsp lemon juice
1 tbsp brown sugar
3 egg yolks
35g caster sugar
50g plain flour
260ml milk
90ml Armagnac or brandy
6 egg whites
$^1/_2$ tsp cream of tartar
pinch salt

Preheat the oven to 180C/350F/Gas4.

Butter the ramekins thoroughly. Be careful that the whole surface is perfectly covered; any gaps and the soufflé will stick and not rise. Place a tablespoon of sugar into one of the buttered ramekins and tap it around the entire surface, making sure that it covers every bit of butter right up to the top. Tip the excess sugar into the next ramekin and do the same, carrying on until all eight are coated.

Place the stoned prunes, apple juice, spices, lemon juice and brown sugar in a small non-reactive pan. Place over a moderate heat and bring the mixture to a simmer. Lower the heat, cover and simmer for 20 minutes, or until the prunes are tender. Add a little water if the pan is drying out. Take off the heat and whiz in the food processor until smooth.

You will be making a thick confectioner's-style custard in a double boiler, so make the following custard base in a double boiler or a large bowl that fits snugly over one of your pans. Place the yolks in the bowl with the sugar and flour. Blend this thick mixture together. Add a few tablespoons of the milk gradually to make a smooth thick just-stir-able sauce base. Heat the remaining milk to just below boiling and pour over the egg mixture, stirring with a wooden spoon, or a whisk. Set the bowl of custard over the pan of shallow simmering water and cook, stirring for 10 minutes or until you have a thick smooth shiny sauce. Take the bowl off the heat and beat in the prune mixture and the Armagnac or brandy. Leave to cool.

Place the egg whites, cream of tartar and salt in your mixing bowl and beat until it reaches stiff, but not dry, peaks. Carefully fold the beaten whites into the prune custard.

Fill the ramekins to no more than two-thirds of the way up the sides. Bake for 20 minutes. Do not open the oven door before this time has elapsed. Eat immediately with cream or chilled *spiced plum sauce* (page 124).

makes 8 individual soufflés depending on ramekin sizes

kouign amann (breton butter cake) with cinnamon

I make no apologies for including another caramel and cinnamon recipe. Such is my admiration for this most successful of unions, I could produce a whole book of them.

Kouign Amann is my 'grail' of bakery. Made from just flour, sugar and the finest salty Breton butter, there is simply nothing else quite like this caramelised, toothsome, dense yet puffed-up confection. One of the greatest culinary mysteries, Kouign Amann originated in a small Breton town called Douarnenez. Unfortunately for all of us, it seems that this recipe has been protected since 1860 by a magic circle of near-Masonic *patissiers* and *boulangers*. Since my discovery of this heavenly yeast cake almost 30 years ago, I have followed a number of dead trails. Here is my current best shot, elaborated (or contaminated) with the rich flavour of cinnamon (please don't tell the *citoyens* of Douarnenez). Not the 'Veritable Kouign Amann de Douarnenez', but still heaven with an appley glass of rough Breton *cidre doux*.

You will need a 28cm flan tin. No loose bases, as you need to contain the butter.

butter for greasing the tin
400g strong white flour
1 x 7g sachet dried yeast (or 20g fresh yeast)
1 tsp sugar
275ml warm water (approximate)
1 level tbsp freshly-ground cinnamon
250g sugar
250g the finest salted butter you can find, softened
1 egg yolk forked up with 1 tbsp water

Line the tin with buttered baking paper.

Mix the flour with the yeast and the teaspoon of sugar in a large warm bowl. Mix in the warm water, or enough to make a malleable, but not sticky dough, and stir with your hand. Pull the dough together and knead lightly for a couple of minutes until it is fairly smooth. One of the secrets of a successful Kouign Amann is not to overwork the dough. Leave to rise in a warm place for 45 minutes or so, or until almost doubled in size.

Mix the cinnamon with the sugar. Beat back the dough and roll it out into an approximate 25cm square, around 1cm thick. Spread with the butter and with 150g of the cinnamon-sugar. Fold two edges to the centre, making a rectangle. Fold the short sides in over each other, making a square again. Cover with a damp cloth, and leave in a cool place to rest for 20 minutes. Not the fridge, as this will firm up the butter too much, making it rupture the dough when you roll it out again.

Pat any air out of the dough again, and roll it out, this time into a rectangle. Sprinkle over half of the remaining cinnamon-sugar mixture. Fold the short sides of the rectangle in over each other, cover and leave in a cool place for a further 20 minutes. Pat and roll out the dough again into a rectangle. Holding back one tablespoon of the cinnamon-sugar, sprinkle the rest over the dough and fold the short sides in again. If the butter is peeping through the dough, sprinkle with flour to prevent it from sticking to the rolling pin. Place the dough in the prepared tin and using the flat of your hand, push it out to the full size of the flan tin. The butter may be seeping through the dough by now, but it doesn't matter. Score the surface at 4 cm intervals in a criss-cross pattern. Brush with the yolk and water mix and sprinkle over the final tablespoon of cinnamon sugar. Leave to rest for a further 20 minutes. Preheat the oven to 180C/350F/Gas4

Bake for around 30 minutes, or until well browned. Serve just warm, or at room temperature with Breton cider.

serves 8

spiced dessert cakes and tarts

When fruit or toffee plays a part in a cake recipe, my spice alarm rings. Bananas? – cardamom. Oranges? – coriander. Apples? – cinnamon, nutmeg, cloves.... A shake of spice sets a cake out in a different direction all together.

cox apple streusel cake with speculaas
orange and almond cake drizzled with coriander atter syrup
yoghurt plum cake with pecans and spices
heady bramley apple upside-down cider cakes
cherry and nutmeg clafoutis-style cake
butternut cheesecake with a ginger crust
moist banana, cardamom and poppy seed cake
chestnut and chocolate caramel spice cake
caramelised apricot and honey upside-down cake
torte de pane (italian spiced bread and butter cake)
glazed marmalade ginger spice cake
yorkshire curd tart
creamy custard and nutmeg tart

cox apple streusel cake with speculaas

Apple desserts always get me shuffling the bottles around in the spice cupboard. This is a light, moist cake with a crunchy buttery topping. It's great as it is with a cup of coffee, or upgrade it to a warm dessert with a swirl of *dark ginger syrup* (page 123) and a spoon of crème fraîche.

Speculaas powder is a warming, aromatic Dutch spice concoction used liberally in the Netherlands in biscuits and cakes (see *nutmeg*, page 30). There are as many speculaas mixes as there are Dutch bakers; below is my favourite balance.

With its lighter spicing, this is a favourite with children. Try making individual cakes in a 12-cup muffin tray (decreasing the baking time to 20–25 minutes) and serve warm with custard or Greek yoghurt.

You will need an 18–20cm loose-based cake tin.

for the speculaas spice mix
1 tsp ground ginger
2 tsp freshly-ground cinnamon
$1/4$ tsp freshly-ground cloves
4 cardamom pods, seeds only crushed in a pestle and mortar
$1/2$ tsp freshly-grated nutmeg
$1/4$ tsp freshly-milled white pepper

for the cake
butter for lining the cake tin
110g salted butter, room temperature
110g caster sugar
1 large egg, lightly forked
225g plain flour
2 tsp baking powder
100ml milk
250g cox apples, peeled, cored and diced to 1cm pieces
60g sultanas

for the streusel topping
30g flour
20g salted butter, room temperature
10g unrefined brown sugar
$1/2$ tsp freshly-ground cinnamon

Preheat the oven to 170C/325F/Gas3. Butter and line the cake tin with buttered baking paper.

Mix the speculaas spices together in a small bowl.

for the cake

Cream the butter and sugar together until pale and light. Add the egg and beat well. Sift in the flour with the baking powder. Add the speculaas spices and all the other ingredients and stir well. Pile the mixture into the prepared tin and smooth over the top.

for the streusel topping

Place the flour and butter in a bowl and rub the butter in with your fingertips until it resembles rough breadcrumbs. You don't need the finest crumb, as the occasional bump is attractive once the cake is baked. Stir in the sugar and cinnamon. Scatter this 'streusel' over the top of the cake.

Bake for around 50 minutes, or until a skewer inserted into the heart of the cake comes out clean. Check after 30 minutes and if the cake surface is picking up too much colour, reduce the temperature slightly. Serve as suggested above.

serves 8

orange and almond cake drizzled with coriander atter syrup

This is a miraculously easy recipe. Toasted coriander boosts and adds an aromatic edge to orange. The polenta gives a unique 'crunch' to the interior of the cake. For a fantastic pudding, serve warm on a shallow pool of *pomegranate and rosewater sauce* (page 123) with a scoop of crème fraîche or Greek yoghurt.

Atter is a blossom syrup of Middle Eastern origin. It's best made at least a few hours, if not a few weeks ahead. It is used for soaking those wonderful nutty pastries, such as baklava. Here it adds another dimension to the cake. Use sparingly if you are also using the pomegranate and rosewater sauce. The atter keeps very well for months in the fridge so don't feel you have to use it all.

Be careful with the orange flower water. It comes in different strengths depending on quality. It also rapidly loses its potency once opened. Add a teaspoon at a time and taste as you go.

You will need a 24cm loose-based cake or flan tin.

for the atter syrup
2 tsp coriander seed
100g sugar
100ml water
1 tsp lemon juice
2 tsp orange flower water, or to taste

for the cake
butter for lining the cake tin
250g salted butter, room temperature
250g caster sugar
1 level tbsp coriander seeds
3 large eggs
2 tbsp orange flower water
220g ground almonds
zest of 3 oranges
1 level tsp baking powder
125g fine polenta

to make the atter

Toast the coriander seeds in a hot frying pan, shaking to prevent burning. Crush them lightly in a pestle and mortar.

Heat the sugar, water and lemon juice in a non-reactive pan. Don't let the syrup boil before the sugar is dissolved. Add the crushed coriander and simmer for 15 minutes or so. Take off the heat and add the orange flower water to taste. Leave to cool. Store in the fridge in a sterilised jar.

to make the cake

Preheat the oven to 170C/325F/Gas3. Butter and line the cake tin with buttered baking paper.

Beat the butter with the sugar for 3–4 minutes, or until the mixture becomes pale and light.

Meanwhile, toast the coriander seeds in a pan over a medium heat, shaking from time to time to prevent burning. Grind finely in your spice grinder, or in a pestle and mortar.

Add the eggs to the butter-sugar mixture, one at a time, beating well between additions. Slow down the beating dramatically and add the other ingredients one by one in the order given, making sure that each is combined before adding the next.

Bake in the oven for 35–40 minutes, or until a skewer comes out of the cake clean.

While still warm, pierce the cake's surface at 4cm intervals with a skewer. Drizzle over a few tablespoons of the atter. Leave for at least 30 minutes for the atter to be absorbed. Serve as suggested above.

serves 8–10

coriander

A mild spice, floral, sweet, aromatic, with a substantial edge of burnt orange, coriander would usually be employed as part of a spice mix reserved for savoury dishes. Here it enhances a sweet orange-flavoured cake and elsewhere works in perfect harmony with other spices in a syrup (*favourite spice syrup*, page 120).

The mellow flavour of the seed contrasts strongly with the astringency of the leaves, but is related through the citrus flavour. As with many spices, the seeds benefit enormously from dry-toasting in a pan.

Coriander is one of the most ancient spices. It has been found in Egyptian tombs taking us back as far as 2000BC. Doubtless in those days it will have been used not only to pep up the royal cuisine, but also in unguents, poultices and love potions. It is grown everywhere. I've even seen coriander grown in fields in West Yorkshire.

Do not buy coriander in a supermarket. Buy a bag of whole seeds at your nearest Asian supermarket. If kept airtight, the seeds suffer little from being stored for a year or so.

yoghurt plum cake
with pecans and spices

Plums, nuts and spices all caramelised together in a moist light cake. Serve with thick Greek yoghurt and a smug grin. And a drizzle of spice syrup never goes amiss. You could also use peaches or apricots.

You will need a 22–24cm loose-based cake tin.

butter and flour for lining the tin
150g salted butter
300g caster sugar
3 large eggs
125g full-fat Greek yoghurt
zest of 2 lemons
2 tsp freshly-ground cinnamon
$^1/_2$ tsp freshly-grated nutmeg
$1^1/_2$ tsp ground ginger
175g self-raising flour
500g plums
1 heaped tbsp pecan pieces
1 tbsp soft brown sugar

Preheat the oven to 170C/325F/Gas3. Butter and line the base of the cake tin with baking paper. Butter the paper and dust the whole tin lightly with flour.

This recipe has a low fat to sugar ratio, so please do use an electric mixer. Beat the butter with the sugar for 3–4 minutes, or until the mixture becomes quite pale. Add the eggs one at a time, beating well between additions. Slow down the beater and stir in the yoghurt and lemon zest. Mix the spices together in a small bowl. Add about two-thirds of the spice mix to the batter with the flour. Fold everything together and scrape into the prepared cake tin.

Halve the plums and take out the stones. If using large plums, cut the fruit into quarters. Arrange the plums, flesh side up, over the top of the cake, right up to the edge, and scatter over the pecans. Mix the tablespoon of brown sugar with the remaining spice mix and sprinkle it evenly over the top of the cake.

Bake in the oven for 50 minutes to an hour, or until a skewer comes out of the cake clean. Serve as suggested above.

serves 8

heady bramley apple
upside-down cider cakes

Crisply caramelised around the rim, these
heady, intensely appley puddings make a
delicious autumn dessert. The cinnamon binds
the sharp appley tang to the sweetness of the
sugar. You could make one large one, but you
get more caramelised rim per serving using
smaller ramekins – and that has to be good.

Please stick to Bramley apples; their
acidity and mealy texture make this dessert.
Serve with a good crème fraîche (not the
average supermarket slime) or ideally
clove and maple syrup ice cream (page 51).

You need six 9cm diameter ramekins.

butter for lining the ramekins
350g Bramley apples
120g soft brown sugar
2 tbsp calvados or brandy
120g salted butter, room temperature
120g caster sugar
2 large eggs
1 tsp baking powder
200g plain flour
1 tsp freshly-ground cinnamon
200ml sweet cider

Preheat the oven to 180C/350F/Gas4. Butter
the ramekins.

Peel, core and cut the apples into 1cm dice.
Place them in a bowl and toss them with the
soft brown sugar and calvados or brandy.

Beat the butter with the caster sugar for
3–4 minutes, or until the mixture becomes
pale and light. Add the eggs one at a time,
beating well between additions. Slow down the
beater and sift in the baking powder with half
of the flour. Add the cinnamon and pour in the
cider. Add the rest of the flour and mix until
smooth, but do not over-mix.

Divide the marinating apple between the six
ramekins, sharing the juices equally. Top with
the cake batter. Bake for 20–25 minutes, or
until firm to the touch and nicely browned.
Cool for 10 minutes or so before inverting the
cakes onto dessert plates.

serves 6

cherry and nutmeg clafoutis-style cake

Nutmeg with a sweet eggy pudding, nutmeg with cherries – this very straightforward dessert has to be in my top ten.

Authentic clafoutis contains more milk. With apologies to French traditionalists, this lies somewhere between a clafoutis and a cake. I think it's the best of both worlds.

Try also with blackberries, blackcurrants or other berries.

You will need a 24–26cm loose-based flan tin.

butter for lining the flan tin
600g dessert cherries, pitted
1 tbsp kirsch or eau de vie
3 large eggs
110g caster sugar
150g plain flour
generous pinch salt
$1/4$ tsp freshly-grated nutmeg
180ml whipping or single cream
generous grating of nutmeg
caster sugar to finish

Preheat the oven to 170C/325F/Gas3. Butter and line the flan tin with buttered baking paper.

Place the cherries in a bowl with the kirsch or eau de vie and put to one side.

Whisk the eggs with the sugar for a minute or so, until pale and well combined. Sieve in the flour with the salt. Add the nutmeg and cream and stir the whole thing together. You will have a fairly slack batter. Strain and scatter the cherries over the base of the prepared tin. Stir any residual juice and kirsch into the batter and pour the batter over the cherries. Grate more nutmeg to taste over the top. Bake in the oven for 40–50 minutes, or until patchy golden brown and firm to the touch in the centre. The mixture will rise slightly around the cherries.

Remove the cake from the oven and dredge with caster sugar. I love my nutmeg, so always give the pudding an extra grating hot from the oven. Leave to cool slightly and serve warm with cream.

serves 8

butternut cheesecake with a ginger crust

A luscious relation of the all-American spiced pumpkin pie, this surprising dessert is great on its own, served with *small dried fruits in spiced syrup* (page 43), *oranges preserved in brandy and spiced syrup* (page 116) or *dark ginger syrup* (page 123).

You will need a 24cm loose-based flan tin.

for the base
110g digestive biscuits
110g ginger biscuits (*world's best ginger biscuits* page 90, or bought)
75g salted butter
40g soft brown sugar

for the butternut cream cheese mix
1 x 700–750g butternut squash
  (about 550–600g flesh)
3 tbsp water
2 tbsp maple syrup
1 heaped tsp freshly-ground cinnamon
$1/4$ tsp freshly-ground cloves
$1/2$ tsp freshly-ground allspice
1 tsp ground ginger
400g cream cheese
250g crème fraîche
100g caster sugar
40g soft brown sugar
large pinch salt
2 large eggs, lightly beaten

for the base

Finely crush the biscuits and place in a bowl. Melt the butter and add to the biscuit crumbs with the sugar. Mix well. Tip the mixture into the flan tin and press it down evenly. Place in the fridge to harden.

for the butternut squash

Preheat the oven to 180C/350F/Gas4.

Peel and deseed the squash and cut into approximate 4cm chunks. Place in a bowl and toss with the water, maple syrup and spices. Transfer with all the liquid to a non-reactive baking tray. Cover with foil and bake in the oven for 45 minutes. Leave to cool. Blend until smooth in a food processor.

to complete the cheesecake

Reduce the oven temperature to 140C/275F/Gas1.

Beat the cheese with the crème fraîche, sugars and salt until well blended. Beat in all but a tablespoonful of the cooled butternut purée and the beaten eggs. Pour over the prepared biscuit base. Stir and swirl the retained tablespoon of squash purée into the surface of the cake. Place in the oven with a small pan of hot water on a lower rack. The water helps to prevent a tough skin from forming over the cheesecake. Bake for about 45–55 minutes, or until the edges of the cake are risen, but the centre is still a touch wobbly. Be careful not to overcook the cake.

Leave to cool and serve at room temperature or colder with a spoonful of fruits in syrup and a swirl of cream if the mood takes you.

serves 8

moist banana, cardamom and poppy seed cake

This cake is packed with bananas giving its intense flavour and delicious dense texture. I'd quite happily eat through one without the icing, but the addition of the topping does catapult this confection into the universe of historic cakes.

You will need a 24cm loose-based baking tin.

for the cake
butter for lining the tin
140g salted butter, room temperature
150g caster sugar
1 large egg, forked
225g self-raising flour
1 heaped tsp bicarbonate of soda
8 cardamom pods, seeds only, crushed in
   a pestle and mortar
$1/2$ tsp freshly-grated nutmeg
2 tsp freshly-ground cinnamon
30g poppy seeds
4 ripe medium-sized bananas, mashed
3 tbsp milk

for the topping
150g cream cheese
50g salted butter
75g icing sugar
1 tbsp lemon juice
2–3 tsp milk
30g banana chips, crushed (optional)

to make the cake

Preheat the oven to 170C/325F/Gas3. Grease and line the cake tin with baking paper.

Cream the butter and sugar in a large mixing bowl until pale and light. Beat in the egg, combining well. Sift in the flour and bicarbonate of soda. Add the spices and the poppy seeds, mashed bananas and milk. Using a large spoon, gently fold all the ingredients together until well combined. Pour the mixture into the prepared tin and bake for 45–50 minutes, or until a skewer, when inserted into the heart of the cake, comes out clean.

to make the topping

Save your arms and use a food processor or mixer to soften and blend the cream cheese with the butter. Add the icing sugar and lemon juice and whiz up again. Add enough milk to give a soft and light texture. Spread over the top of the cooled cake. Sprinkle with the banana chips, if used.

serves 8

chestnut and chocolate caramel spice cake

This is my Christmas cake. It has all the tastes of Christmas, with chocolate as a bonus. And the chestnuts, as well as having a great mellow flavour, give a moistness and a crunch at the same time. I've simply never understood the big appeal of the traditional dense, sometimes dry, showy-offy, fruit-packed, plaster- and play-dough-coated confection. And of course you can make this dense, fudge-topped, moist-yet-crunchy, rich-yet-light spice cake any time.

Make the cake a day in advance of the icing; it holds together better on splitting to ice the middle.

You will need a deep loose-based 26cm cake tin.

for the cake
butter and flour for lining the tin
225g salted butter, room temperature
110g white fat, room temperature
375g soft dark sugar
170g caster sugar
5 large eggs
350g plain flour
70g cocoa powder
1 tsp baking powder
3 tsp freshly-ground cinnamon
$^3/_4$ tsp freshly-grated nutmeg
$^1/_4$ tsp freshly-ground cloves
225ml milk
200g tinned chestnuts
for the chocolate frosting
75g salted butter
40g cocoa
35ml milk
350g icing sugar
for the spiced fudge frosting
65g salted butter
135g sugar
135g brown sugar
65ml evaporated milk
1 tsp freshly-ground cinnamon

to make the cake

Preheat the oven to 170C/325F/Gas3. Butter and line the cake tin with buttered baking paper. Flour the inside of the tin. Beat the butter and fat with the sugars for 3–4 minutes, or until the mixture becomes paler and quite light. Add the eggs one at a time, beating well between additions. Sift in the flour, cocoa and baking powder. Add the spices and fold into the mixture with the milk. Blend the chestnuts in a food processor until they resemble fine breadcrumbs and add to the mix, combining well. Scrape the mixture into the prepared cake tin. Bake for 70–90 minutes, or until a skewer inserted into the heart of the cake comes out clean.

to make the chocolate frosting

Melt the butter over a gentle heat. Do not allow it to sizzle. Add the cocoa and cook, stirring for a minute or so. Take off the heat and beat in the milk and icing sugar.

to make the spiced fudge frosting

Place all the ingredients in a pan over a low heat. Stirring, allow the butter and sugars to melt before the mixture simmers. Cook for a couple of minutes, stirring. Take off the heat and leave to cool for 10 minutes or so and then beat until it thickens slightly.

to assemble the cake

Once it has cooled, or preferably the next day, slice the cake in half horizontally. You would be well advised to slide a flat baking sheet under the top half to remove it; this cake is very moist and will crumble and break easily. The frostings spread most easily when they are just warm. If either frosting stiffens, you can reheat them very gently for a more manageable texture. Spread and swirl either or both frostings onto the bottom half of the cake and return the 'lid'. Spoon, swirl, spread or drizzle the frostings over the top as you like. Any old fool can make this cake look great.

makes a large cake for 16–20

caramelised apricot and honey upside-down cake

Still warm from the oven and served with a generous swoosh of cream this has to be one of my favourite puddings. It looks stunning and every mouthful has its own individual but delicious personality. The juicy tartness of the apricots contrasts perfectly with the comfort of the moist, spiced honey cake. And the whole cake is rimmed by the most delicious, spicy chewy caramel.

The cake comes alive in the oven, rising and falling as the apricots and caramel bubble away.

make the most of your honey!

Measure the honey first and then the hot water in the same receptacle; the water will rinse out any honey dregs.

You will need a 22–24 cm cake tin.

butter for lining the tin
for the caramel
75g salted butter
130g soft brown sugar
for the cake
2 tbsp flaked almonds
60g crystallised ginger, thinly sliced
400g apricots, halved, stones removed
50g salted butter, room temperature
25g white fat (or another 25g butter), room
  temperature
75g caster sugar
1 large egg
230g plain flour
1 tsp baking powder
small pinch salt
2 tsp freshly-ground cinnamon
1 tsp ground ginger
zest of 1 lemon
100ml honey
100ml hot water

to make the caramel

Butter and line the cake tin with one large disc (approximately 35cm in diameter) of baking paper so that the base and the sides are covered. The paper disc must be large enough to contain the bubbling caramel.

Melt the butter and sugar in a small non-reactive pan over a gentle heat. Do not allow the caramel to boil before the sugar and butter are both melted. Simmer for a couple of minutes and pour directly into the lined cake tin. Tip the tin from side to side to make sure that the base is totally covered.

to make the cake

Preheat the oven to 180C/350F/Gas4.

Scatter the almonds and sliced ginger over the caramel and arrange the apricot halves, cut side down on top. Beat the butter, white fat and sugar until light and quite pale. Beat in the egg. Slow down the beating and sift in half of the flour, the baking powder and salt. Add the spices, lemon zest and honey with the rest of the flour. Finally pour in the hot water. Mix until smooth, but do not over-mix.

Spoon the cake batter over the apricots. Bake for 35–40 minutes, or until a skewer comes out clean from the centre of the cake. Leave to cool for 15 minutes before turning out onto a plate.

serves 8

torte de pane (italian spiced bread and butter cake)

A delicious spiced variation of the ubiquitous but very special Italian pudding-cake originally designed to use up old bread. The finished cake is a distant, firmer and rather sophisticated relation to our own bread and butter pudding.

You will need a 20cm loose-based cake tin. The tin must be at least 7cm deep, as the torte rises significantly during baking, though it falls back once taken out of the oven.

butter for lining the tin
3 tbsp grappa, kirsch or eau de vie
40g sultanas
generous pinch of saffron, ground in a pestle and mortar
250g day-or-two-old good white bread, sliced and crusts removed
75g salted butter, room temperature
350ml milk
150ml double cream
120g sugar
zest of 1 lemon
zest of 1 orange
$1/4$ tsp freshly-ground cloves
1 tsp ground ginger
1 tsp freshly-ground cinnamon
45g crystallised ginger, chopped small
30g pine nuts, toasted
4 large eggs, separated
icing sugar for dusting

Warm the grappa gently in a small pan. Place the sultanas and the saffron in a bowl and pour over the grappa. Leave to soak for at least one hour.

Preheat the oven to 170C/325F/Gas3. Butter and line the cake tin with buttered baking paper.

Dry out the bread for 5–7 minutes in the oven. Tear the bread into a bowl and mix with the butter. Place the milk and cream in a pan and bring to the boil. Pour straight over the bread and butter and beat until fairly smooth. Allow to cool. Stir in the sugar, zest of lemon and orange, the spices, crystallised ginger and pine nuts. Finally pour in the soaked sultanas and saffron with the grappa. Add the egg yolks and mix very well. In a separate clean bowl whisk the egg whites until stiff, but not breaking up. Fold the whites gently into the mixture. Pour the mixture into the prepared tin.

Bake for about one hour, or until a skewer inserted into the heart of the cake comes out clean. If the top of the cake is browning deeply before the cake is cooked, cover the top with a piece of foil.

Allow to cool for 15–20 minutes before removing from the tin. Dredge with icing sugar. Serve warm.

serves 8

glazed marmalade ginger spice cake

I've always loved ginger cake. Even the stick-to-the-roof-of-your-mouth blocks out of a packet. But if you make your own, you can take control of the ground ginger jar and add an extra hot gingery kick. Orange marmalade adds a tasty and sticky dimension.

You will need a 20 x 30 cm cake tin, or equivalent.

for the cake
butter for lining the tin
90g salted butter
150g golden syrup
200g orange marmalade
240g self-raising flour
4 tsp ground ginger
2 tsp freshly-ground cinnamon
2 large eggs, lightly forked
120ml milk
2 tbsp brandy or dark rum

for the glaze
2 oranges
4 tbsp ginger syrup from jarred crystallised ginger or 2 tbsp honey and 2 tbsp orange juice heated with a $^1/_4$ tsp of dried ginger
3 tbsp brandy or dark rum

for the cake

Preheat the oven to 170C/325F/Gas3. Butter and line the cake tin with buttered baking paper.

Melt the butter with the golden syrup in a non-reactive pan. Take off the heat and mix in the marmalade. Sift the flour into a mixing bowl and add the spices. Stir in the warm mixture and then add the eggs, milk and brandy or rum. Combine well and pour into the tin. This is meant to be quite a runny mixture, so don't be alarmed.

Bake for 25–30 minutes, or until firm to the touch in the centre. To be sure, check that a skewer piercing the middle of the cake comes out clean. It is very important not to over-cook this cake, as a dry ginger cake is charmless.

for the glaze

You will be pouring the glaze over the cake while it is warm, so prepare it while the cake is baking. Using a zester, pare thin strips off the oranges. Place the zest in a small non-reactive pan and blanch in a little boiling water for 5 minutes. Strain and repeat the blanching process two more times. This process takes the bitterness out of the zest.

After the third blanching, place the zest back in the pan and add the ginger syrup and brandy or rum. Simmer for a couple of minutes.

to finish the cake

When the cake comes out of the oven, pierce with a fine skewer at 4cm intervals. Gently pour over the hot glaze making sure that the entire surface is covered. If the zest is in a tangle, spin it out with a fork.

Allow to cool and serve as a cake or as a pudding with thick cream.

serves 8

yorkshire curd tart

I just had to include this. This is Yorkshire sugar and spice at its homely best. Great with a mug of tea after you stumble off the moors. The best tarts are reputedly made using curds made from the richest custard-yellow milk of a newly calved cow. Delicious to be sure, but this recipe is lighter than the original sometimes found propping doors open in traditional Dales tearooms. Here, we blind-bake the pastry for a crisper result, and the mix is lighter and slimmer than our stout Yorkshire ancestors would have it.

You will need a loose-based 26cm flan tin.

for the pastry

160g plain flour
40g salted butter, chilled and diced
40g white fat, chilled and diced
approximately 2 tbsp ice cold water
1 egg white, forked for brushing

for the filling

225g curd cheese
100ml double or whipping cream
85g caster sugar
100g dried fruit – sultanas, mixed dried fruit,
   chopped apricots, etc.
45g white breadcrumbs
1 tbsp flour
pinch salt
2 large eggs plus 1 egg yolk
$1/2$ level tsp freshly-ground allspice
zest of 1 large lemon
1 tbsp caster sugar for sprinkling

to make the pastry

You can make the pastry by hand, but I prefer to use the food processor. Place the flour in the processor with the butter and white fat. Pulse the processor until the mixture resembles breadcrumbs. Tip into a large bowl and add enough water to achieve a soft, but not sticky dough. Put in a plastic bag and leave in the fridge for at least 45 minutes.

Remove the pastry from the fridge 20 minutes before you need it.

Preheat the oven to 180C/350F/Gas4. Roll the dough out on a floured surface to a thickness of around 3–4mm and large enough to fill the flan tin. Ease the pastry into the tin. Fold excess pastry back into the tin, pressing it down against the outside of the ring. The sides of the pastry case will thus be thicker than the flat base. Once you have pressed the pastry against the sides, it should be about 5–6mm thick. There will still be excess pastry standing up above the level of the tin. You will be trimming this during baking. Line the pastry with a disc of baking paper and fill with baking beans. Bake for 10–12 minutes, or until the pastry is firm and barely beginning to brown. Remove from the oven and lift out the baking paper with the baking beans. Using a serrated knife, trim the pastry to the level of the top of the tin. Prick the base a few times with a fork and bake for a further 5–10 minutes, or until the pastry case is golden and crisp. Remove from the oven and brush with the egg white. Return to the oven for 1 minute to seal the base. This helps block the fork holes and prevents the pastry from becoming soggy when you pour in the filling.

to complete the tart

Reduce the oven temperature to 170C/325F/Gas3. Beat the curd cheese well with all the other ingredients bar the caster sugar for sprinkling. Pour the mixture into the still-warm baked pastry case and bake for 25–30 minutes, or until the filling is risen, and beginning to brown. Remove from the oven, leave to deflate and cool for 10 minutes or so and then sprinkle with caster sugar.

Serve warm with a swoosh of cream, or allow to cool before serving with a mug of tea.

serves 8–10

creamy custard and nutmeg tart

Please don't turn the page! Nutmeg and sweetened egg make perfect partners. And here they combine in their simplest form. Custard tarts you have eaten in your time may have left you with a memory of cold, thick, lardy pastry holding an eggy slab. But when well made, it makes the most delicious dessert. With light fine crisp pastry, a slim layer of enriched custard filling and a generous grating of nutmeg, it is an elegant revelation.

You will need a loose-based 26–28cm flan ring.

for the pastry
160g plain flour
40g salted butter, chilled and diced
40g white fat (or more butter if you prefer), chilled and diced
scant 2 tbsp ice-cold water
1 egg white, forked, for brushing

for the filling
300ml milk
300ml double cream
1 vanilla pod, or a few drops of good vanilla extract
3 large eggs
2 large egg yolks
75g sugar
generous grating of nutmeg

to make the pastry

Follow instructions for *yorkshire curd tart*, page 82.

to fill the tart

Reduce the oven temperature to 170C/325F/Gas3.

Pour the milk and cream into a pan. If using the vanilla pod, split it lengthways with a small sharp knife and add it to the pan. Bring the pan steadily to the boil and allow to simmer gently for 10 minutes or so to infuse the vanilla. Remove the vanilla pod from the pan and place it on a plate. Using the rounded point of a table knife, strip out the tiny seeds. Being careful not to lose any, whisk the seeds into the pan. Meanwhile, place the eggs and yolks in a bowl and break them up using a spoon rather than a whisk (you don't want to introduce too much air). Add the sugar and combine well. Pour in the creamy vanilla milk and mix well.

To prevent spilling, fill the pastry case while it is standing on the oven shelf. Strain the egg custard mixture through a coarse sieve into the case. Grate generously with nutmeg and bake to 45–55 minutes, or until set. If there is a slight wobble in the centre, that's fine. It will set as it cools. Whatever you do, don't let it soufflé or rise; the egg mixture will split.

Leave to cool and serve as it is, or with a dribble of cream.

serves 6–8

allspice

Allspice is so named as it seems to carry the aromatic oils of a number of spices, including cinnamon, nutmeg and cloves, in one handy, hard, round, reddish-brown package. It looks like a large peppercorn. In fact, many have mistaken it for pepper; thus its Spanish name 'pimienta', the French 'piment de Jamaique' and not forgetting the Yorkshire name, 'clove pepper'. In reality it is the dried berry of a tree grown in Jamaica and South America. It also grows naturally in rainforests, where it is harvested and sold by locals.

Its aroma is warm, pungent and almost savoury. When ground and toasted, it reeks of Christmas. It has strong preservative properties and is used in everything from perfumes to flatulence tonics. Like all spices, you can buy it ground, but this is one of those spices that loses aroma very rapidly. The moment you open the jar, you're losing those aromatic oils.

spiced biscuits, muffins and bread

Something spiced for your cup of tea.

raspberry and cinnamon breakfast muffins
light spice sablé biscuits
macadamia nut, orange and star anise biscotti
world's best ginger biscuits
cinnamon and walnut biscuits
cornish saffron spiced fruit bread

raspberry and cinnamon breakfast muffins

Like any muffins, these are really chuck-them-together easy and best fresh from the oven. Crisp yet chewy on the top, packed with breakfast ingredients and harbouring a jammy secret, they will go down well with everybody, either with a spoonful of Greek yoghurt or just as they are with a cup of coffee.

Ingredients pick out different notes in spices. Here the raspberry jam brings out the citrus side of cinnamon. Try these and you'll see what I mean.

You will need a 12-cup muffin tin.

butter or oil for greasing muffin tin
160g flour
110g sugar
100g breakfast cereal, crushed (e.g. Shreddies, Bran Flakes, Special K)
3 tsp baking powder
$^1/_4$ tsp salt
1 tsp freshly-ground cinnamon
180g low-fat yoghurt
2 tbsp honey
55g salted butter, melted and cooled
2 large eggs, lightly forked
80g/12 tsp raspberry jam
1 tbsp breakfast cereal, crushed
1 tbsp Demerara sugar
$^1/_2$ tsp freshly-ground cinnamon

Preheat the oven to 190C/375F/Gas5. Lightly grease your muffin tin.

Mix together the first six dry ingredients in one bowl and the yoghurt, butter and egg in another. Add the mixed dry ingredients to the wet and stir to combine well.

Place one dessertspoonful of the mix into each muffin cup and spread across the base of the cup with the back of the spoon. Place a teaspoonful of the jam on the centre of the mix in each cup and then cover with the remaining muffin batter making a sealed pocket of jam.

Mix together the tablespoon of crushed cereal, Demerara sugar and the $^1/_2$ teaspoonful of cinnamon in a small bowl. Sprinkle this mix over the muffins. Bake for 15–20 minutes, or until the muffins are firm to the touch.

Turn the muffins out onto a cooling rack. Serve warm, but be careful, the jam in the centre may be hot.

makes 12 muffins

light spice sablé biscuits

Subtle, buttery and delicious, these biscuits make a great accompaniment to any spiced fruit compote, but they are tailor-made for *spiced cherry sablé* (page 40).

2 egg yolks
$1^1/_2$ tbsp whipping cream
65g icing sugar
130g salted butter, room temperature
185g strong white flour
pinch baking powder
1 generous pinch freshly-ground cloves
$^1/_2$ tsp freshly-ground cinnamon

Beat the yolks with the cream and icing sugar in a mixing bowl until well combined. Add the butter and beat well. Sift in the flour and baking powder. Add the spices and combine to make a soft dough, but don't over-handle. Place the mixture in a plastic bag and refrigerate for at least 2 hours.

Remove the pastry from the fridge at least 20 minutes before using.

Preheat the oven to 180C/350F/Gas4. On a well-floured board and using a well-floured rolling pin, roll out the dough to a thickness of about 3–4mm. Cut out rounds of 7–8 cm diameter and transfer to baking sheets. Bake for 7–9 minutes, or until just browning around the edges. Leave to cool for a few minutes before transferring to a cooling rack.

makes approximately 18 biscuits

macadamia nut, orange and star anise biscotti

Many biscotti recipes do not contain butter and can leave you with something as hard and tough as old dog biscuits. These classy twice-baked biscuits are crisp and buttery with a firm whiff of aniseed and the tang of orange. Delicious with a glass of sweet wine, or dipped into *peaches and raspberries in chilled spiced frascati* (page 10).

Maybe if star anise weren't so perfect and magically beautiful in its intact state, it wouldn't taste so good. Maybe I've fallen under its spell, but I find that these immaculate stars carry a sweeter, more penetrating, aromatic and warmer flavour than any other aniseed spice. The fennel seeds you'll often find studding biscotti can be pretty obtrusive.

butter for lining the baking sheet
110g salted butter, room temperature
170g caster sugar
2 large eggs
2 tbsp brandy
340g plain flour
$1/2$ level tsp freshly-ground star anise
$1^1/_2$ tsp baking powder
zest of 1 large orange
100g macadamia nuts, roughly chopped

Preheat the oven to 180C/350F/Gas4. Lightly grease a baking sheet.

In an electric cake mixer, beat the butter with the sugar for 3–4 minutes, or until the mixture becomes quite pale. Add the eggs one at a time, beating well between additions. Stop the machine and add the other ingredients. Turn the beater back on to a very slow speed and mix until all is well combined.

Tip the dough out onto a floured work surface. Divide the dough into two and roll each half into cylinders 3–4cm thick. Transfer the cylinders to the baking sheet and bake in the oven for 15–20 minutes, or until golden and firm to the touch. Remove from the oven and leave to cool for 5–10 minutes. Carefully transfer to a chopping board and, using a serrated knife, slice the baked cylinders on a diagonal at approximately 1cm intervals. Return the biscotti to the tray. You may need to lightly grease a second tray to accommodate all of them. Bake for a further 12–15 minutes, or until nicely golden and firm to the touch. The biscuits will continue to firm up once out of the oven.

makes about 50 small biscotti

world's best ginger biscuits

Serve with the world's best cup of tea.

110g salted butter
240g caster sugar
1 large egg
2 generous tbsp golden syrup
1 tbsp chopped crystallised ginger
1 tsp freshly-ground cinnamon
240g plain flour
1 tsp bicarbonate of soda
1 heaped tsp ground ginger

Preheat the oven to 150C/300F/Gas2. Lightly grease your baking trays with vegetable oil.

In an electric cake mixer, cream the butter and sugar until light and pale. Add the egg and beat well. Add the syrup, chopped ginger and cinnamon and beat again. Sieve in the flour, bicarbonate of soda and ginger. Mix well together.

Place walnut-sized nuggets of the mixture onto the baking trays, leaving at least 5cm between them; these biscuits spread enormously.
Bake for around 20 minutes. Leave to cool for a few minutes or so before transferring them to a cooling rack. Any longer and you risk them sticking to the tray.

makes 30–35

ground dried ginger

Dried ginger has a peppery, but rounded and comfortable flavour, possibly hotter, but not so acidly sharp and not so lemony as the fresh root. This is the one spice that I would buy ground. I find grinding dried rhizomes hard work. You are invariably left with fibres and lumps. Paler and more aromatic, the best quality ginger is said to come from Jamaica.

cinnamon and walnut biscuits

Crisp, nutty and aromatic, these sophisticated biscuits are from the repertoire of my great friend José Luke, who is one of the best bakers I know. The fridge technique ensures a neat shape every time. Delicious on their own, with a cup of tea, with *poached pears with spiced syrup* (page 14), or with any spiced fruit compote and Greek yoghurt.

225g salted butter
200g caster sugar
100g walnut pieces
1 level tbsp freshly-ground cinnamon
1 large egg yolk
250g plain flour

Place the butter, sugar, walnuts and cinnamon in a food processor and process to a paste. Add the yolk and process again. Now add the flour and pulse until nearly blended. Tip and scrape onto a lightly floured surface and pull the biscuit dough together.

Roll out into a sausage shape and wrap securely in baking paper. Still wrapped in the paper, roll the dough again to achieve a perfectly round sausage, about 6–7 cm in diameter. Refrigerate for at least 1 hour.

Preheat the oven to 170C/325F/Gas3.

Once firm, slice the dough 'sausage' thinly. You can decide on the thickness; I go for 4–5mm. Line baking trays with baking paper and place the rounds on the trays leaving at least 3cm between them. Bake for 10–15 minutes, depending on thickness. Leave to cool for a few minutes before lifting them onto a cooling rack.

makes 40–50 slender biscuits

cornish saffron spiced fruit bread

It is said that saffron was introduced to Cornwall when the visiting Phoenicians traded it for tin. Whether myth or truth, traditional saffron recipes for cakes, buns and breads pop up all over this beautiful county. For me, saffron is too pungent a flavour for cakes; but with its affinity to yeast, it works terrifically well in more feisty and muscular fruited breads. And if you have any leftovers, this loaf makes a revelatory bread and butter pudding.

The quantity of saffron required depends on its quality. This recipe is geared towards top quality threads. See *saffron* (page 96).

for the dough
1 scant level teaspoon saffron threads
1 x 7g sachet dried yeast (or 20g fresh yeast)
1 heaped tbsp sugar
225ml milk, warmed
600g strong white flour
75ml warm water
110g butter, melted and cooled to just warm
2 tbsp sour cream
1 tsp freshly-ground allspice
1 tsp freshly-ground caraway seeds
2 tsp freshly-ground cinnamon
$1/4$ tsp freshly-ground cloves
1 tsp salt
150g raisins
30g mixed peel
for the glaze
50g sugar
50ml water

Grind the saffron threads in a pestle and mortar. Leave to steep in a little hot water for at least 30 minutes. Place the yeast with the sugar and warmed milk in a large bowl and leave in a warm place for at least 5 minutes, or until the mixture starts to froth. Add 500g of the flour to the yeast mixture with the water, melted butter, sour cream, spices, salt and the saffron strands with soaking liquid.

Mix and pull it all together with your hand. Add as much of the reserved 100g of flour as you need to make a soft malleable dough.

Knead the dough for 10 minutes or so, then cover with greased Clingfilm and put in a warm place to rise for an hour or until doubled in size. Knock the dough back and roll out to the size of a large pizza. Scatter the raisins and mixed peel over the centre of the dough and enclose it as if wrapping a parcel. Push and handle the dough to distribute the fruit. Leave it to rest for 10 minutes.

Preheat the oven to 200C/400F/Gas6.

Form the dough into twelve individual buns, a loaf or a plait. If any dried fruit is poking out, prod it back in and stretch a bit of the dough to submerge it back into the body of the bread. Any surface fruit may burn, or swell unattractively. Leave the dough, covered with greased Clingfilm, to rise until doubled in size. Uncover and bake for 10 minutes in the hot oven before reducing the temperature to 180C/350F/Gas4. Bake the loaf for a further 25–30 minutes, or until cooked through. The bottom of the loaf will sound hollow if tapped. For the buns, cook for a further 10–15 minutes.

While the bread is baking, make the glaze by dissolving the sugar in the water in a small pan over a low heat. Bring the syrup to the boil and cook for 2 minutes. The glaze will be brushed over the hot crust as soon as it emerges from the oven.

makes a 1.2kg loaf or 12 lovely buns

saffron

Saffron is quite a particular spice mostly associated with savoury dishes. In some sweet dishes, it seems to be used more for its intense colour than for its rich flavour. Its deep aroma is musky and lingering, honeyed and yeasty with a subtly bitter edge. I wouldn't use it on its own. It can be slightly medicinal and just too odd. But partnered by more rounded spices, such as cinnamon (*cornish saffron spiced fruit bread*, page 94), or with cardamom (*saffron and cardamom ice cream*, page 49), or with the floral tones of rosewater (*sweet and sticky medjool date pudding-cake*, page 62), the beefiness of saffron is tamed.

Saffron threads are the dried stigmas of the saffron crocus. Each flower has just three stigmas. The flowers are hand picked at dawn and dried gently in small quantities on a sort of fine riddle held high over a low flame. You can see why saffron is the most expensive spice in the world. And the best is very expensive indeed.

As with Gucci handbags and Rolex watches, there are many saffron imitations and some pretty convincing to the untrained eye. Watch out for saffron 'special offers'. In my experience there is no such thing. In Mediterranean markets I've seen enormous bags holding 'saffron' in such quantities that if real, you would have to take out a mortgage to buy. I've had earnest tradesmen trying to peddle me yellow flowers. Remember the saffron crocus is violet. If the flowers are yellow, they are more likely to be safflowers. The best quality saffron is bright red; not yellow or reddish-brown. Spanish saffron from the rocky hillsides of La Mancha is said to be some of the best. I buy from an Iranian shop and it's great. Whatever you do, don't buy it in a supermarket; it's just too expensive and have you seen the packaging?

the sweetest
of sugar and spice

Adventures with sugar and spice in small but powerful packages.

glittering indian sweets with saffron and cardamom
spiced banana and coconut wontons in sesame toffee
mr greenwood's cha cha cha chocolate chillies
sugar and spice fudge

glittering indian sweets with saffron and cardamom

Using gold and silver leaf is a delicate business. Your skin attracts these flimsy, gossamer-thin films of precious metal leaving you with gold or silver fingers. Fortunately, they cling with an even greater affinity to these sticky spicy sweets, so with a pair of tweezers, you can make these into literally brilliant confections.

for the sweet mix
110g skimmed milk powder
225ml milk
60g sugar
$1^1/_2$ tbsp double cream
1 tbsp ghee, or melted clarified butter
$^1/_2$ tsp saffron strands, crushed
seeds of 6 cardamom pods, finely crushed

to decorate
2 or 3 pieces gold or silver leaf
3 tbsp mixed chopped nuts or seeds –
   e.g. pistachios, almonds, pine nuts

for the sweet mix

Place all the sweet ingredients together in a bowl and mix together, whisking to get rid of any lumps. Pour into a small non-reactive heavy-bottomed pan. Cook very slowly, stirring to prevent the mixture from catching for 10-15 minutes, or until well thickened to the consistency of a thick béchamel sauce. Take the pan off the heat and turn the mixture out onto a plate to cool.

to decorate

Line a tray with baking paper. When the sweet mixture is just warm and firming up, using a teaspoon, take walnut-sized pieces of the mixture and place them on the paper. Using tweezers, tear and lift pieces of the gold or silver leaf and drape them over the sweets. You will find that the leaf will cling very happily.

Scatter the mixed chopped nuts on a dinner plate. Place the sweets in turn on the plate of chopped nuts, rolling each one to cover any of its surface not coated with silver or gold.

Leave to set for a couple of hours. The sweets will keep very well for a day or so in the fridge.

makes 16 stunning walnut-sized sweets

spiced banana and coconut wontons in sesame toffee

Never used wonton wrappers? Well you've missed one of those brilliant ingredients available from the fridges or freezers of Oriental supermarkets. You can fill them with anything, from abalone to zebra, seal them with water and fry them in oil. Here is a sweet wonton – a cousin three times removed from the ubiquitous Chinese restaurant banana fritter.

If you don't want to go the extra yard and make the sesame toffee, just dredge the fried wontons with caster sugar mixed with some freshly-ground spice.

for the wontons
350g bananas, approximately 8mm dice
1$^1/_2$ tbsp coconut cream, melted in a pan and
    left to cool
zest of 1 lime
3 tsp lime juice
1$^1/_2$ tsp freshly-ground cinnamon
$^1/_2$ tsp ground ginger
$^1/_4$ tsp freshly-grated nutmeg
1 tbsp brown sugar
pinch salt
30 x 7cm wonton wrappers
to fry
300ml groundnut oil
2 tsp sesame oil
for the toffee
300g sugar
3 tbsp sesame seeds

to make the wontons

In a bowl, mix the diced banana with the coconut cream, lime zest and juice, spices, sugar and salt. Try making one wonton to assess the amount of filling required. Lay a wonton wrapper out on the kitchen surface. Place about a level teaspoon of banana filling in the middle of the wrapper. You will be making a little envelope. Wet the edges of the wrapper with water. Fold the top of the wrapper over the filling and the bottom up over that. The water will do the sealing. Flatten and seal the open ends on either side. Wet these ends and, as if wrapping a present, fold the ends in, scrunching a little. Turn the wrapped wonton over and place on a piece of greaseproof paper. Repeat until all the mixture is used up.

to fry

Pour the oils into a fryer, pan or wok. Heat until a little hazy. Fry the wontons several at a time and leave aside on kitchen paper to absorb any excess oil.

to make the toffee

Place the sugar with the sesame seeds in a small pan with a tablespoon of the frying oil. Melt the sugar over a gentle heat, stirring from time to time until dissolved. Add the fried wontons a few at a time to the melted toffee. Cover completely and remove to a piece of greaseproof paper. Serve once the toffee has cooled.

makes approximately 30 wontons

mr greenwood's cha cha cha chillies

It is my great fortune to have Hope and Greenwood, the renowned purveyors of all things sweet and chocolaty, just a trot along the road. Luckily for me, it seems that I have spent enough of my pocket money on sherbet fountains and chocolate gingers to have prized a succulent and thrillingly exciting recipe out of Mr Greenwood, the twinkly-eyed owner with the curlicue moustache.

The red-lipped, kitten-heeled Miss Hope does warn us that Mr Greenwood's white chocolate chillies are wickedly hot, so please do nibble them with caution. Hence the 'Cha Cha Cha' name; Mr Greenwood's chillies take you for a gentle waltz and then dance the Cha Cha Cha with your taste buds. But it's not just the heat that carries you off, just imagine the combination of chilli, lime, tequila, white chocolate and salt. Addictive, tantalising and delicious. Miss Hope suggests serving them as an interesting taste bud twister pre-dinner with cocktails, or in a $9^1/_2$ *Weeks* moment of abandon.

Melting white chocolate is a tricky old business, so please don't knock back too much of the tequila before you have these spicy delicacies on a plate on the sideboard.

With all these recipes, I would usually suggest how many people it might serve, but this one is a little controversial. Some might feel that just a nibble is quite enough, but there are those who would polish off the entire recipe on their own. I'll leave it up to you.

For a neat result, you will need a small piping bag.

6 large red chillies
200ml silver tequila, or enough to cover
  the chillies
125g Valrhona Blanc, finely chopped
  (or similar high cocoa butter content white
  chocolate i.e. at least 30%)
zest of 1 lime
Maldon Salt

Slice the chilli lengthways on one side only. Wearing disposable, or rubber gloves, remove the seeds, leaving a long pouch. Place the deseeded chillies in a small container, pour over the Tequila and soak overnight. This soaking process not only takes some of the 'yeehah' out of the chilli, but also furnishes you with a great chilli tequila cocktail base.

Strain the chillies and put both chillies and tequila aside. Melting white chocolate is a gentle business. It burns, goes grainy and coagulates very easily. Remember: you're not cooking the chocolate; you're just melting it. Bear in mind that chocolate melts in your mouth at around 37C. Find a bowl that will sit snugly over a pan. Place the pan on the heat, without the bowl, containing just a few centimetres of water. Allow to simmer and then turn off the heat. Place just 75g of the chocolate into the bowl. Leave the pan temperature to drop for 60 seconds before placing the bowl on the pan. Slip a wooden spoon in between the pan and the bowl to leave a gap for steam to escape. The chocolate will melt, barely reaching your own body temperature. As soon as the chocolate is melted take the bowl off the pan.

Put a couple of teaspoons of the chilli tequila into a ladle and heat it to body temperature over the gas. This will take about 10 seconds. Carefully test with your finger. Don't heat it any longer or it will flame. Stir the warmed tequila into the melted chocolate with the lime zest. Do not over-stir. You will probably find that the chocolate seizes slightly. Working quickly, scrape the mixture into a small piping bag. Fill each of the chillies generously, from end to end. Refrigerate to set.

Melt the remaining chocolate and scrape it into the middle of the bowl. Drag and roll the chillies through it to coat them. Transfer to a sheet of greaseproof paper and leave to set.

To serve, pop on a plate and sprinkle wildly with Maldon salt.

sugar and spice fudge

There's a rather beautiful lady at our local market who sells the most delectable fudge. At Christmas, she rolls out a spiced version, firm yet creamy, which I adore. Naturally, she won't divulge her recipe, but inspired, I think I've cracked it. Great for presents; even better for you.

One of the secrets of fudge making is in the beating. In an otherwise leisurely activity, this is the point at which you must rouse yourself for action.

You will need a sugar thermometer.

butter to line the baking tray
150ml milk
150ml single cream
570g granulated sugar
450g soft brown sugar
30g finest butter you can find
$1/_2$ tsp salt
1 level tsp cream of tartar
2 heaped tsp freshly-ground cinnamon
2 level tsp ground ginger
$1/_2$ tsp freshly-grated nutmeg
a generous pinch of freshly-ground cloves

Butter a 30 x 20 cm lipped baking tray or similar. Ceramic, plastic, pyrex are all fine.

Pour the milk and cream into a heavy-bottomed non-reactive pan and bring to the boil. Take off the heat and add the sugars, butter, salt and cream of tartar. Place back on the lowest heat possible and stir to dissolve the sugar. The mixture must not boil before the sugar dissolves and the process can take 15 minutes or so. Stir off the heat for a while if you feel the mixture is getting too hot. Scrape crystallised sugar from around the edge of the pan using a straight-sided knife and return it to the mixture to dissolve.

Bring the mixture to a simmer and place the sugar thermometer in the pan. Make sure that the bulb is clear of the bottom of the pan and immersed in the simmering liquid, not just in the foam. Do not stir from this point – or not until I tell you to. Continue to simmer for 15–25 minutes, or until the thermometer reaches 'soft ball', or 116–118C/240–244F/Gas1–2. Turn the heat off at this point. Still not stirring, leave the mixture to cool for 10–15 minutes or so. Then the beating begins.

Add the spices and beat the mixture until it begins to thicken and crystallise around the edges. This can take as long as 15 minutes. Once the crystallisation begins, you have to move fast. At this point, pour the mixture into the prepared tray. Shake the tray to make the fudge level. Leave to cool and slice with a hot knife.

makes 1kg

drinks with spice

From the smooth luxury of hot cinnamon chocolate
to the curative pick-me-up of fruit and ginger juice,
spices have many roles in drinks.

mango lassi with jaggery, ginger and cardamom
curative fruit and ginger juice
hot rocket cider
hot eggnog
hot cinnamon chocolate with cream

mango lassi with jaggery, ginger and cardamom

This sophisticated, light and refreshing Indian drink is utterly delicious and remarkably good for you from brain to liver, particularly if you use live yoghurt. Great on its own. Or turn it into a brilliant dessert with a scoop of *saffron and cardamom ice cream* (page 49) and sprinkle with crushed pistachios or toasted pine nuts.

100g jaggery or unrefined brown sugar
2 large ripe mangos
400ml low-fat live yoghurt
2 tsp finely-grated peeled fresh ginger root
juice of 1 lime
seeds of 8 cardamom pods, crushed in a pestle
   and mortar
300ml water
6 ice cubes

Dissolve the jaggery, stirring over a moderate heat, in a small pan with 4 tablespoons of water. Slice the mango flesh from either side of each mango's flat stone. Cut each piece into thick wedges and remove and discard the skin. Cut the remaining ring of skin from around the stone and discard. Slice off any remaining flesh.

Place all the ingredients in a blender and whiz up until well blended. Serve in tall glasses.

serves 4–6

curative fruit and ginger juice

Once you have a juicer, you soon gather that you can stick anything through it. It's great to experiment, but if you want a guaranteed instant pick-me-up, this is the one for you. For colds, for exhaustion, for energy....

2 cox apples, washed
1 ripe mango, peeled and sliced
30g fresh ginger, scrubbed
200g carrots, scrubbed
6 stems mint
6 stems parsley

Push all the above through your juicer for an all-day pick-me-up.

serves 1–2

hot rocket cider

My husband Nige and I ran a stall at Glastonbury Festival in 1997. That was one of the muddy years. Opposite was a mulled cider tent. We looked on ruefully through the drizzle at the snaking queue, which persisted from one morning to the next morning and then to the next. Hot, spiced cider warms you to the core. And I tell you, their recipe wasn't a patch on this one.

Just remember, the longer you simmer, the less alcoholic it becomes.

2.5 litre bottle cider
30cm cinnamon sticks
$1/2$ nutmeg, lightly pounded
6 cloves
1 strip red chilli (no seeds)
6cm chunk fresh ginger, peeled and roughly
  chopped
3 strips orange zest
120ml brandy or rum
freshly-squeezed juice of 1 lemon (or to taste)
brown sugar to taste

Simmer the cider with the spices, chilli, ginger and orange zest for 20 minutes. Add the brandy or rum and simmer for a further 5 minutes.

Add the lemon juice and sugar to taste.

You can strain it if you like, but this mixture isn't too pungent with spices, so you could just serve it from the pan and leave the bits bobbing around to be sieved out with your teeth.

other great additions

Instead of brandy, try Calvados, Triple Sec or ginger wine.

hot eggnog

The heady hit of brandy and the warmth of nutmeg running through this frothy creamy cupful wrap you in a blanket of comfort and reassurance. This is a cosy fur-lined boot to the stiletto of Zabaglione.

As an alternative, try the recipe substituting with Calvados and cinnamon.

450ml milk
2 freshest eggs
1 pinch salt
60g caster sugar
120ml brandy
freshly-grated nutmeg to taste

Pour the milk into a small pan and heat gently while you prepare the egg base.

Whisk the eggs and salt vigorously in a large bowl for a minute or two, or until thickening. Add the sugar and beat for a further minute. Warm the brandy gently in a small pan.

Pour the hot milk and warm brandy over the egg mixture and beat well. Grate in a little nutmeg and stir. Pour the eggnog into warmed mugs and grate over a further sprinkling of nutmeg.

serves 4

cardamom

Cardamom has a very distinct and quite unique flavour. Rather like bergamot or fresh coriander, the first taste can be too much of a shock to win you over; but gradually it grows on you until you are addicted. Most of India is; it is everywhere in its cuisine, from sweet rice puddings to savoury dals. So for good prices and freshness, look no further than your local Indian supermarket.

Cardamom is expensive, falling just short of the A-list world of saffron and vanilla. This is because the pods are hand picked with expertise. The pods on one bush ripen at different times and the timing of picking is key. They must be almost, but not quite ripe. If the pods burst, they are worthless. They are dried quickly to keep the seeds tightly packed and to retain their aromatic oils in the safety of the rough outer husk.

For sweet dishes, you need the more delicate green cardamom with its warm lemony pungent fruity flavour with an edge of eucalyptus. The oval shaped pods are triangular in cross-section and house three inner chambers that contain tightly packed seeds. This is where the flavour lies. And the stickier the seeds are, the fresher the spice is, the more aroma hits you.

hot cinnamon chocolate with cream

Very very simple, but utterly delicious.
It's a Mexican tradition to team cinnamon with chocolate. The two flavours meet in the middle with a dusky twang.

100g high cocoa content chocolate
200ml water
800ml milk
80g caster sugar
pinch salt
1 tsp freshly-ground cinnamon
4 tbsp whipped cream

Break up the chocolate into the water in a medium-sized pan and heat gently to melt the chocolate. Do not let it get anywhere near boiling. Heat the milk to just below boiling in another pan and add to the chocolate with the sugar, salt and all but a sprinkling of the cinnamon. Pour the hot chocolate into the mugs and top with cream and a final sprinkling of cinnamon.

serves 4

spicy jars

A few stunning jars, glinting with colour and floating with spices. Make great gifts – or keep them all to yourself.

fresh ginger and rose petal jelly
apple and chilli jelly
oranges preserved in brandy and spiced syrup

fresh ginger and rose petal jelly

The prettiest pinkest thing you ever did see. Delicious on ice cream, scones and of course toast. And more interestingly, as mint jelly is to roast Welsh or Yorkshire lamb, the clear sharp aromatic flavour and aroma of ginger and rose petal jelly is to Middle Eastern spiced lamb.

You'll find the dried rose petals in Middle Eastern stores.

100g fresh ginger root, scrubbed and roughly
   chopped
300ml water
90ml freshly-squeezed lemon juice
780g sugar
85ml liquid pectin
3 tbsp dried rose petals

Sterilise your jars and lids in boiling water and then dry them in the oven.

Using a food processor, blend the ginger with half of the water. Once the ginger and water are well puréed, add the remaining water and blend again. Strain through a sieve; pressing on the ginger to obtain the last drops. Leave to stand for at least one hour for the sediment to settle.

Transfer the ginger juice steadily to a measuring jug, leaving the sediment behind. Make the volume up to 425ml and transfer to a small non-reactive pan. Add the lemon juice and bring to the boil. Add the sugar, allow it to dissolve and bring to a rolling boil. Add the rose petals and pectin and simmer for one minute. Pour directly into the sterilised jam jars.

The rose petals will tend to float. As the mixture cools, stir with a sterilised metal spoon every 20 minutes or so, until setting begins in earnest, to redistribute the rose petals.

makes approximately 1kg

apple and chilli jelly

This makes a great relish, striking both to the eye and the palate, for cheese, cold meats and as a condiment for barbecued, roasted or grilled meats over which it will melt alluringly.

If you've never tried it, this is a thoroughly delicious, simple and cheap way of introducing yourself to the craft of jelly-making. The natural pectin and acidity of the apples are sufficient for a good set.

It's always difficult to predict the heat of a chilli, but I do prefer this jelly to have a good bite, which is promised by the following recipe.

You will need a jelly bag.

1kg Bramley or very tart apples
1 litre water
2 large red chillies
white sugar

Sterilise your jars and lids in boiling water and dry them in the oven.

Wash and chop the apples into chunks, removing the stems, but retaining the skins and cores, and place in a non-reactive pan with the water. Chop the stem off the chillies, slice them lengthways and leaving in the seeds and pith, add them to the pan. Bring to a gentle boil and simmer until soft. For a successful jelly, you need to release as much of the acid and pectin from the fruit as you can. This process is helped if, as the apple begins to soften, you press it with the back of a wooden spoon to help break down the pulp: 10-15 minutes should do the trick.

Pour the warm pulp into a jelly bag and let it strain until no more juice drips. Don't be tempted to squeeze. Measure the volume of juice and weigh out 400g of sugar for each 500ml of juice. Return the juice to the preserving pan. Add the sugar and dissolve slowly before the pan boils. Meanwhile remove the chillies from the apple pulp, rinse them under a tap and remove any seeds. If you have a wand blender, whiz the chillies with a few tablespoons of the liquid until almost smooth. Alternatively, pound to a paste in a pestle and mortar before adding them to the boiling pan. Boil rapidly until set. Setting time will vary enormously from 5 minutes to 20 minutes, depending on pectin content and acidity of the fruit. Test for setting after 5 minutes by allowing a spot of the jelly to cool on a plate. When, on cooling, it forms a skin, is tacky and gives the suggestion of a wrinkle when pushed with a fingertip, the jelly is ready to pot and cover. Pour into warmed sterilised jam jars. Cover the surface with waxed paper and lid. Do not disturb the jars until they are cold.

makes 1kg

oranges preserved in brandy and spiced syrup

This semi-preserve is exceptionally pretty and leaves a tang and a zing on the tongue. It is delicious with a spoonful of Greek yoghurt or can be strewn over cakes, creams and puddings. Try with *sweet and sticky medjool date pudding-cake* (page 62) or with *panna cotta* (page 31).

Make sure that you use small thin-skinned oranges.

1kg small oranges
150ml white wine vinegar
100ml brandy
100ml water
500g sugar
30cm cinnamon stick
2 tsp coriander seeds
6 pieces star anise
6 cloves
6 slices fresh, peeled ginger root

Sterilise your jars and lids in boiling water and then dry them in the oven.

Slice the oranges into 5mm thick circles, discarding the fleshless ends. Put the sliced orange into a stainless steel pan and pour over enough water just to cover. Place over a moderate heat and bring to the boil. Turn the heat down, cover and simmer gently for about an hour, or until the skins are well softened. Carefully strain the cooked orange, discarding the orange water. This may seem surprising, but if you were to taste it, you would see why.

Pour the vinegar, brandy, water and sugar into the pan and dissolve the sugar over a low heat. Once dissolved, add the whole spices and ginger and bring the syrup to the boil. Simmer for 10 minutes. Add the oranges and cover. Lower the heat and simmer very gently for 20–30 minutes, or until the fruit is becoming slightly translucent.

Using a slotted spoon, transfer the cooked fruit to the warm, sterilised jars, holding back the spices as much as you can. Pour over the hot syrup and distribute the spices attractively around the sides of the jars.

Keeps well in the fridge for months.

makes approximately 1 litre

star anise

Originally from China, but now grown all over the Far East and into India, this most beautiful of spices grows as an eight-pointed seedpod on a species of evergreen Magnolia.

These dusky brown stars with their shiny seeds nestling within look beautiful bobbing around in fruit syrup with oranges, and also in *favourite spice syrup* (page 120). Ground star anise imparts a penetrating, sweet and fresh liquorice aroma, brilliant in biscuits (*macadamia nut biscotti with orange and anise*, page 89) and as part of a warming spice mix in any cakes or puddings. Interestingly, our feline friends like it too – it is frequently found as a constituent of cat food.

sauces and syrups

A small collection of delicious sauces to coat steamed puddings, ice cream, pancakes or thick yoghurt.

favourite spice syrup
spiced caramel syrup
pomegranate and rosewater sauce
dark ginger syrup
gingery calvados caramel sauce
apricot sauce
spiced plum sauce

favourite spice syrup

A spice syrup is very pretty. It is also delicious for pouring over ice creams, steamed puddings, cakes, dribbling into coffee, over rice pudding, Greek yoghurt, custards, pancakes... the list goes on. There's always one in our fridge. This has to be one of my favourites, but the room for improvisation is copious.

375g sugar
500ml water
$1/4$ tsp salt
20cm cinnamon stick
3 pieces star anise
3 cloves
2 tsp pink peppercorns
2 tsp coriander seeds
6cm chunk fresh ginger, peeled and finely sliced
4 long strips finely pared lemon rind
2 tsp dried rose petals or 2 tsp rose water
  (optional)
2 tbsp freshly-squeezed lemon juice (or to taste)

Place the sugar, water and salt in a non-reactive pan. Allow the sugar to dissolve over a low heat before the syrup simmers.

Add the spices, fresh ginger and lemon rind and simmer for 10 minutes. Add the rose petals or rose water while the syrup is still bubbling and then take the pan off the heat.

Add fresh lemon juice to taste just before serving.

makes about 600ml

spiced caramel syrup

A richer and more characterful sauce for ice cream and the rest.

250ml *favourite spice syrup* (see above)
75ml water

Strain the syrup into a non-reactive pan, retaining the spices. Place over the heat and bring to a simmer. The syrup will already be a pale amber colour. You will need to simmer without stirring until it is bubbling and

approaching a dark amber colour. This should take 12–15 minutes. At this point, taking great care, pour in the water. The pan will spit and crackle shockingly, so take a step back as soon as you pour the water in. Once it has calmed down, carry on stirring over the heat to get rid of any lumps. Take off the heat and return the retained spices to the pan. Transfer to sterilised jars.

makes about 300ml

sumac

Like lemon juice in the West, sumac is basically an acidulating flavour enhancer used in the Middle East. It is the ground, dried berry of a Mediterranean bush and has an orange-red colour. It is both cooked into dishes and used as a table condiment. The whole dried berries can be hard to find, but ready-ground are available at all Middle Eastern stores.

pomegranate and rosewater sauce

A very simple, sweet and sharp sauce related to me by an old Iranian friend and a delicious match for sugary Middle Eastern-style puddings and cakes. Perfect with *orange and almond cake* (page 68).

You can buy pomegranate juice and rose water in Middle Eastern stores.

100g caster sugar
2 tsp cornflour
240ml sweetened pomegranate juice

$1/2$ tsp rose water

Place the sugar and cornflour in a small stainless steel heavy-bottomed pan. Pour over the pomegranate juice and whisk to get rid of lumps. Place over a moderate heat and bring to the boil, stirring constantly. Simmer for a minute or so, or until the mixture thickens and clears. Add the rose water and combine. Serve hot or cold.

makes 250ml

dark ginger syrup

I'm not sure if I should reveal this, but this recipe was inspired by school dinners. The inventive dinner ladies at my middle school came up with a memorable spicy syrup recipe to pour over ginger sponge. The recipe below is pretty true to my memory. Try it poured over steamed sponge pudding or *cox apple streusel cake* (page 66).

210g sugar
270ml water
4cm chunk ginger, peeled and finely grated
large pinch salt
juice of $1/2$ lemon

Place the sugar with half of the water in a pan. Heat gently to dissolve the sugar, stirring to accelerate the dissolving process. Once dissolved, bring the syrup to a simmer. Do not stir from this point, but watch the caramelisation process carefully. When the syrup is a rich caramel colour, taking great care, pour in the remaining water. The pan will spit and crackle shockingly, so take a step back as soon as you pour the water in. Once the pan has calmed down, carry on stirring over the heat to get rid of any lumps. Add the ginger and place the pan back on the heat. Simmer gently for 5 minutes. Stir in the salt and lemon juice. Take off the heat and leave to cool and thicken.

makes 250ml

gingery calvados caramel sauce

A thick butterscotch sauce. Delicious on ice cream and steamed puddings. Also fantastic made with brandy, rum or whisky.

$2^1/2$ tbsp Calvados
140g salted butter
70g soft brown sugar
$2^1/2$ tbsp double cream
1 tsp dried ground ginger

Place all the ingredients in a heavy-bottomed, non-reactive pan over a slow heat and allow to melt and blend together before the mixture reaches a simmer. Simmer gently, stirring continuously for two minutes. Take off the heat and leave to cool and thicken.

makes 250ml

apricot sauce

Whiz up one recipe quantity of *fresh apricot compote* (page 37), adding water to obtain the required consistency. Serve with *medjool date pudding-cake* (page 62) or *caramelised apricot upside down cake* (page 78).

spiced plum sauce

Whiz up one recipe quantity of *spiced plum compote* (page 35), adding a little water if necessary. Serve with *prune and armagnac soufflé* (page 63).

shopping for spices

Any well-stocked Asian, Far or Middle Eastern high street store will stock most of the spices used in these recipes. (See introduction, *how to buy, use and look after spices*, page 7). If you are not lucky enough to live close enough to such a shop, there are many excellent spice suppliers on the internet. At the time of print, the sites below offered the best value and were the most reliable, but new sites are popping up all the time.

Some supermarkets will stock larger bags of spices at reasonable prices in their 'ethnic' or 'food from around the world' aisles. However, these stores will invariably be located in areas with a heavily ethnic demographic, where the high streets will already be peppered with specialist stores.

SMBS Foods
75 Lordship Lane, East Dulwich, London SE22 8EP (020 8693 7792).

My personal favourite; these guys sell everything and more in a 'tardis' of a high street health-orientated delicatessen/grocer. The range of spices is terrific and as a supplier of the obscure and the wonderful, they take some beating.

The Spice Shop
1 Blenheim Crescent, London W11 2EE (020 7221 4448)
www.thespiceshop.co.uk

Birgit Erath of The Spice Shop has dedicated the past fifteen or so years to a spice Odyssey, finding small suppliers and individual small farms all over the world to stock her breath-taking and highly aromatic Notting Hill store. She will always buy in whole spices; seed, bark, pod or whatever form they take. No fumigation, no irradiation. She stocks absolutely everything, whole or ground and also grinds her own fresh blends.

Persepolis
28-30 Peckham High Street, London SE15 (020 7639 8007)

Persepolis is a charming shop and is my preferred supplier of sumac and saffron. Packed with Persian goodies from hubble-bubbles to belly dancing garments, from baklavas to sugared nuts and fruits, they also have every spice named in this book at fantastic prices.
Sally Butcher, proprietor, is incredibly helpful, knowledgeable and full of Peckham buzz. She will willingly mail-order.

www.seasonedpioneers.co.uk

For well-sourced spices and spice mixes from an adventurous and passionate supplier, try Seasoned Pioneers. A beautiful and informative website.

www.saltandpepper.co.uk

There's nothing these people don't know about pepper. This website provides a good range of spices, but is most interestingly a peppercorn specialist stocking what must be one of the widest range of country of origin peppercorns around. They also make their own exhilarating peppercorn blends.

www.thespiceoflife.co.uk

For an encyclopaedic and competitively priced supplier, promising everything from Allspice to Zedoary Root.

index

thanks

Endless thanks to:

Mum and Dad; José Luke; Miss Hope and Mr Greenwood; Rijka Van Engelen; Blistering Barbecues; Meg, Matt and Jon at Absolute Press; Jason; And my gorgeous family.